Contents

All About Matt

Matt is best known as the agony uncle for Bliss and AOL, and as a frank spokesman on teen and relationship issues. He has written numerous health awareness campaigns, for Radio One, The Health Education Authority and Brook Advisory, and was an advisor on youth issues to the Government's Chief Medical Officer.

Matt would especially like to thank all those who were so open about their parents' separation or divorce. Without their contributions, this book would never have been written. Some names have been changed but they know who they are. Also thanks to Polly and Marina for getting the ball rolling.

INTRODUCTION

For every five marriages that set sail, two of them are likely to hit the rocks ...

This means that nearly a quarter of all children up to sixteen years old will see their parents' marriage founder. That's a big figure. So if you're one of that number, remember –

you are not alone...

My mum and dad are still married. At school, this made me feel like the odd one out. So many of my mates had parents who'd split up that I was almost embarrassed to admit that I hadn't witnessed any dramatic family bust-ups. I even considered inventing some kind of parental tension to get a vote of sympathy from the girls! After all, it seemed to me that having divorced parents somehow qualified you to frown and look moody when it suited. Another plan was to refer casually to my mum and dad by their first names, because that's what people with step-parents did. That, to me, sounded cooler than an ice-cream in winter.

What I didn't realise, however, was that the people I envied had each gone through the hardest emotional upheaval of their lives. The truth of this came home one lunch break when the canteen discussion got on to the subject of divorce. Everyone involved, apart from me, either lived with a single parent or in a stepfamily, and so each had a different experience to relate. I didn't say a word, for what I heard was both shocking and enlightening.

For an hour they talked, swapping stories about their parents' separation. Some tales made us laugh, others invited fierce disagreement or sympathetic nods. One girl unthreaded a tale so knotted up with emotion it held everyone within earshot spellbound. Everyone involved saw themselves in these stories, and it helped them to make sense of their personal experiences. When the bell rang for the next lesson and we all went off to our different classes, it was clear to me that I was not the only one who had learned a thing or two that lunch break.

Packed with invaluable help and information about dealing with your parents' divorce, this book also features first-hand advice from people like you – teenagers who have been where you stand now, and who have gone on to develop a strong and positive outlook on life. With this book and their help, you can do the same.

CHAPTER ONE

Mum and Dad are splitting up

Perhaps you've opened this book feeling that your whole world has come apart at the seams. Why? Because you've just found out that your parents have decided to go their separate ways.

The news might have come as a surprise. For others, finding out that their mum and dad are splitting up can be less of a shock. Often it just confirms the suspicions that they've had for ages.

"When they tell you it feels like you're watching a movie that's part fact and part fiction. There's something about it that you just can't believe."

Imogen (16)

"I didn't ask any of the questions I wanted to ask when my parents broke the news, probably because I was so embarrassed talking about things like love with them. We'd never even got on to the subject of relationships before!"

Lloyd (17)

"Just after my parents told me they were separating, I went out and called on a friend. I didn't let on anything was wrong because I was trying to block it out of my mind."

Alice (14)

Learning that your parents no longer want to be with each other is a moment you never forget. It's one that leaves you reeling with confused emotions and unanswered questions.

Right now, let's try to make sense of those emotions and deal with the questions often asked when parents split up. You may not find the solutions to all of your problems, for every divorce is different just as no two families are the same. It's tough at the beginning, but with support and understanding you will get through the experience and learn to get on with your life. To kick off, let's look at life before everything turned pear-shaped.

Not so happy families

"It was always the same. My parents would row, stop talking to each other and then make friends again. This went on for years, but every time it would take longer for them to make up. Eventually, they stopped talking altogether and Dad moved out."

Jake (15)

Have you ever met a family that never argues, always smiles, and never frowns, sulks or shouts? Okay, so they're ten-a-penny on TV, but we're talking about the real world here.

In reality families like this don't exist. The stresses, strains and pressures of everyday life are just too difficult to contain without someone snapping occasionally and taking it out on the people they live with.

Too close for comfort?

"Mum and Dad used to fight more on holiday than when they were at home. I think it had something to do with the fact that they weren't able to get away from each other for a whole fortnight!"

Caroline (16)

Anyone with a brother or sister will know how easy it can be to wind each other up. You know how it goes – you argue at breakfast, sulk with each other through supper and then wrestle for the TV remote until one of you snaps. Often it's just because you're sharing the same space.

It's only when you spend less time cooped up together that you start to get on again. Maybe then you can even share a laugh! But though they're often the last person in the world you want to see, they will always remain your brother or your sister. Nothing can change that.

The same goes for you and your parents. If their marriage breaks down they can get divorced, which means they stop being husband and wife. But although one of them may go off and live with someone else, she or he will always be your mum or dad; their feelings for you will remain as strong as before.

Sometimes, parents find they get on much better once they're living apart. Alternatively, a couple who split up may choose never to see each other again.

What's certain, however, is that if you're living in a seriously unhappy home then a separation or divorce can make for a more peaceful, hassle-free life for everyone. The snag is this takes time.

Parents are people

"What made their split so hard for me to handle was that my mother had fallen in love with another man. You just assume that your parents will only ever have eyes for each other."

Nathan (15)

We don't choose our parents; there is no catalogue from which we can make a selection. Our parents decided to have us. We didn't have a say in the matter. As a result, most of us take our parents for granted at times and assume they were put on this earth just to wash our clothes, feed us, and embarrass us in front of our mates. The fact that they have interests other than us is unthinkable!

But remember, parents are also people. And when they admit things aren't working out between them, you're forced to look at them and their relationship in a different way. You have to accept that they are individuals with needs, desires and interests. Sometimes their outlook on life conflicts, leading them in different directions.

Yes, they used to love one another and share each

other's lives. Now things have changed, and if they're going to be happy then they have to go their separate ways.

Once news of their separation is out in the open, you will at least know the score. In many ways life before this can be even harder to deal with if you know something's wrong between your mum and dad but no one tells you.

Of course, it's possible for news of the split to come as a total surprise. In many cases, however, people suspect long before that not everything was sweetness and light between their mum and dad. All too often a nagging suspicion will have worked its way into your head.

 *"I never heard my parents arguing. Instead, they just seemed to be in a permanent sulk. Sometimes I thought it was because of something I'd done wrong. It was only when they told me they were splitting up because Dad loved another woman that everything fell into place."*

Toby (15)

Am I to blame?

"I went clubbing one Friday night without telling my parents where I was going. Mum was a bit cross when I got back, but when Dad told her to go easy she went berserk with him. They ended up rowing most of the weekend, which made me feel completely awful!"

Ralph (16)

When you're not sure what's wrong, it's easy to assume all kinds of terrible things about the state of your mum and dad's relationship. It's also very easy to blame yourself. Don't. The truth couldn't be more different.

Looking after a teenager may not be a breeze but whatever grief you have caused your parents, even if your room's so disgusting the dog won't step inside, it won't be enough to drive them apart. Whatever has been responsible for your mum and dad's split, you are not to blame.

Why won't they say what's going on?

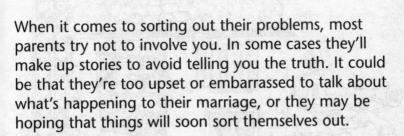

"Sometimes I'd ask Mum what she and Dad had been arguing about. Every time she'd say it was nothing. It made me more certain that some major hassle was going on between them."

Donald (16)

When it comes to sorting out their problems, most parents try not to involve you. In some cases they'll make up stories to avoid telling you the truth. It could be that they're too upset or embarrassed to talk about what's happening to their marriage, or they may be hoping that things will soon sort themselves out.

Some parents may have convinced themselves that you haven't noticed anything is wrong. But no matter how much your mum and dad try for your sake to keep you in the dark, all too often the reality of the situation is crystal clear. And all you really want is for your parents to sit down with you and talk your worries through.

My home's a war zone!

"Things got so bad between my parents that I was embarrassed to bring mates home in case we walked in on an argument."

Jay (14)

Marriages can break down for many different reasons but just before they split, there's nearly always an air of conflict in the way parents behave.

Arguments

> "My parents were like ticking time-bombs. As soon as Dad came home each evening I'd see Mum tense up. This was my cue to leave and go to my room."
>
> Fiona (14)

Let's face it, everyone has their bad days. You. Me. Arsenal FC. Your mum and dad, too. Even parents who are madly and passionately in love can find faults in each other that drive them up the wall. Yet sometimes a row can be good for a relationship. Shouting, cursing or throwing a tantrum can be a great way of letting off steam. Unfortunately, if the marriage is already in difficulties, some parents find it almost impossible to kiss and make up.

Parents argue over many things. They might stop seeing eye-to-eye on major subjects that just can't be avoided. Issues like money, jobs and houses are often the cause of big bust-ups as they affect the whole family.

On the other hand, your mum and dad may fall out over things that appear to you to be really trivial. It might seem a bit over the top when your parents argue about the housework or whose turn it is to walk the dog, but in many cases these are signs of deeper tensions. The truth often remains unspoken.

Stroppy silences

"For about a year or more before the divorce my mum and dad would go quiet whenever I walked into the room. If they believed that I hadn't sussed something was up they must have thought I was from Mars!"

Harriet (15)

Some parents go to great lengths to hide their problems. But even if your mum and dad disagree about every subject under the sun, including the weather, there will always be one thing they'll still agree on, and that's your happiness.

Often this means they agree not to argue when you're around. In reality, however, most people find it hard or even impossible to switch out of a row at a moment's notice and then pretend nothing's wrong. Your parents might have your interests at heart, but when it's clear that they're itching for an argument it can create a tense and uncomfortable atmosphere for everyone in the family.

In many ways an uneasy silence can affect you more than a spectacular row. Two people glowering at each other can ruin your appetite, prevent you concentrating on homework, or make watching the TV a less-than-enjoyable experience. At least when they're arguing and airing their problems you get a chance to learn that you're not to blame for their troubles!

Constant criticism

"Dad couldn't walk through the door without being nagged. Mum would always find something bad to say. Looking back I see it as proof that they weren't getting on, and not the reason why they finally split."

Warren (15)

You know how annoying it can be when your parents do it to you:

'Turn that down!', 'Stop slouching!', 'Move that school bag!' Feeling criticised all the time can really wind you up, especially when you think it's unnecessary. Nobody likes being told what to do, and it can make you feel as if that person has no respect for you. Tension and even anger can build up until the only way to let it all out is to shout and scream.

So what makes one parent criticise the other? Often it's because they know the other almost too well. Having lived together for so long, your mum and dad know each other's every habit – even the annoying ones. When they first got married, your mum may have silently tolerated the way your dad left his stinky socks on the bedroom carpet. It may seem like nothing, but even something as silly as that can blow up out of all proportion if they're not getting on well. This then becomes the focus for all the problems in their relationship.

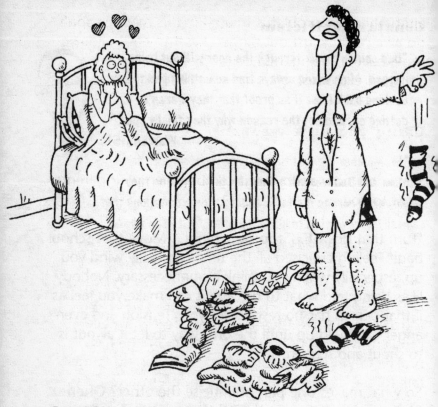

Avoiding one another

"Dad spent more and more time away on business – he was hardly ever at home. After Mum finally explained that they didn't love each other anymore, he stopped coming home altogether."

Siri (16)

Some parents find it easier to pretend their problems don't exist rather than to face up to them. They will avoid the whole issue by avoiding one another. What's more, some parents stay out of each other's way so much that they can even stop communicating altogether. But problems treated in this manner don't go away – they just get bigger. Resentment builds up like a balloon being inflated, and eventually the situation explodes.

Using you as a weapon

"I remember the last time we ate together as a family. Mum and Dad weren't talking by then. Instead they glowered across the table and asked me questions that really they wanted to ask each other. If it hadn't been so upsetting I would have told them both to get a life!"

Jenny (17)

Let's be absolutely clear. If your parents can't live together any more then they must deal with the problem without using you. If their marriage has broken down to the point where they can no longer talk to one another, never let them use you as a go-between.

Sometimes it's hard not to agree to pass messages to and fro, especially when you feel it might eventually get your mum and dad talking to one another again. But as soon as you begin dashing back and forth you're more than likely to get caught in the cross-fire. One parent may think you're taking sides, for example, or even deliberately start to use you against the other, which is totally unacceptable.

If you feel you're being used as a weapon, disarm yourself. Tell them you think they are placing you in an impossible position, and you are not prepared to do it. Speak up for yourself, not for your parents.

If your mum and dad need a mediator there are many professional organisations that can help (see Chapter Ten).

Violence

"I was in bed at the time, but I could hear my parents shouting and things being smashed in the living room. It was really scary, even though I knew they'd never hurt me."

Andrew (15)

Violence can be responsible for your parents' separation, or a result of the pressure of their relationship breaking down. Either way, it's a tragic thing to happen in any home. Witnessing your parents fighting can be very distressing.

Some marriage problems may have affected one parent so deeply that violence is the only way they can express their anger or unhappiness. It may be extremely out of character, and you may be surprised as well as frightened if one of them becomes physically abusive. Often it's the last resort before a separation.

In some sad cases a parent might be abusive towards their partner, or even the whole family, as a way of controlling them. But violence has no place in any home. A split is often the best thing for everyone.

If you need to talk, but feel unable or embarrassed to discuss the situation with your mum and dad, you must speak to someone you trust. A family friend or relative, a teacher or a school counsellor can give you support and advice.

Not every marriage breaks down into violence or abuse, just as not all mums and dads shout at one another or use you as a weapon. Some parents may simply drift apart, and decide that living separately would be the most positive way for each of them to get on with their lives.

Once your parents have agreed to separate, this is usually the time they take a deep breath and tell you what's going on.

We have something to tell you . . .

"I knew what they were going to tell me. I could see it in their faces when they asked me to sit down. As soon as Dad said he was leaving home, all I could say was: 'I know.'"

Theo (15)

No parents want to admit to their children that their marriage hasn't worked out. Put yourself in their shoes. To them it can feel like admitting they've failed you. As a result, coming clean can be one of the toughest things your mum and dad will ever do.

Some parents rehearse how they will tell you about the divorce. They'll be totally prepared to help you and able to explain in practical terms how the split will affect you and the rest of the family. Sadly, however things don't always run so smoothly.

Sometimes the separation can come as a complete shock to one parent. This often happens if the other parent has announced out of the blue that he or she is leaving, perhaps for someone else. If your dad has just walked out, for example, then your mum may have no choice but to tell you what's happened before she has had a chance to deal with her own emotions. It may also take some time before she actually accepts that he's not coming back. At a stage when you need support, you end up providing a shoulder for someone else to cry on.

What's the story?

"When Mum told me Dad had abandoned us and gone to live on his own, I knew there was more to it than that. Dad had telephoned earlier and explained that he still loved me but Mum had asked him to leave."

Simon (16)

Try to make sure your parents are completely straight with you. If their marriage has broken down badly, one of them may try to blame the other or distort the facts. They may not set out to tell you half truths or only half the story, but sometimes it can be difficult for your mum and dad to give you a balanced and complete explanation.

So, before you take sides find out the other side of the story. The responsibility for most divorces must be shared between parents, and not blamed on one of them. There's always one thing that both parents will agree played no part in causing the split – and that's you.

> "I felt left out when my parents first told me about their plans, but I suppose I understood that there wasn't much I could have done to keep them together. What was more important to me was the fact that I could talk to them afterwards and understand why they'd split."
>
> Natasha (15)

If your parents are too upset to listen to you, or you'd just prefer to talk to someone neutral, find a relative or a friend whose parents have already divorced. It's down to you to speak up and talk to someone who can identify with your feelings.

Your mum and dad will already know your view about their separation. After all, it's only human nature for us to want our parents to stay together forever. But as your parents probably realised early on, and as we'll see in the next chapter, staying together for your sake isn't always the best way forward.

CHAPTER TWO

So you thought you had problems

Just for a moment, let's travel back through the mists of time to the day your parents got married.

Imagine how your mum and dad felt when they looked into each other's eyes and declared their vows. It would have seemed impossible for them to live without each other. Neither could imagine a future when it would be impossible for them to live with each other!

Even if your parents no longer get along, it's worth remembering that they got married with the best intentions in the world; they wanted to be together for the rest of their lives. Sadly, nobody can be certain what the future will bring.

People change. Couples can either adapt and stay together, or drift apart when their attitudes, hopes and desires change. This can put a strain on any marriage, and often something in that relationship snaps. But even separating parents who can't bear to share the same air space will always be bound together by their children.

Good times, bad times

"Seeing my mum and dad split up means I've seen the down-side of marriage. It's not put me off the idea of getting married but it has made me aware that things can go wrong. One lesson I've learned is – never pick on your partner at breakfast. It always leads to a bust up!"

Elizabeth (15)

"My parents divorced five years ago. Their marriage ended badly and now they don't have much to do with each other. The funny thing is that when I see them separately, both still talk about what great family holidays we had when I was a kid."

Paddy (17)

When people announce that they are getting married, their friends and family are thrilled. It's a time for celebrations all round. Ask them why they're getting hitched, however, and most will find it hard to give you an answer.

Sure, they'll stare dreamily into each other's eyes and say they love each other to bits, but for most couples the decision to marry is simply the next natural step forward in their relationship. Basically, they each see their future enriched by being together.

It's those who have already experienced married life who can offer words of wisdom. "It won't be easy," they say. "You have to work hard to make a marriage work." But what kind of work do they mean?

Making a marriage work

> "Slowly Mum and Dad stopped doing little things for each other, like making the tea or going out for meals together. It was as if neither of them could be bothered any more."
>
> Serene (14)

Making a marriage work means working for each other. Like running a three-legged race, a husband and wife have to get into step with each other or risk falling over. It's rewarding when it works, but if one partner pulls too hard or the other doesn't make enough effort, then both are likely to fall flat on their faces. Here are some things that married couples have to be aware of if their relationship is going to succeed. They have to know:

- what makes the other person happy.

- what makes the other person angry.
- when the other person needs a helping hand.
- when the other person needs space.
- when to accept the blame.
- when to say sorry.
- that sometimes it's best to forgive and forget.

Marriage means that each partner has to learn to live as one half of a couple without losing their individuality, interests and identity. Married couples have to be able to talk through their feelings and know when to compromise when they can't agree.

Sounds hard, doesn't it? But if you think about it good friendships need to follow the same principles, so we can all practise with our friends first!

What's love got to do with it?

"Mum and Dad stopped kissing each other goodbye about two years before they separated."

Kerry (15)

It's especially tough to get your head around how love works because people show their feelings for each other in very different ways. Some couples are lifelong romantics, and so when love leaves home it's obvious. Others prefer to keep their love to themselves. This means it can be almost impossible for you to know exactly how your parents feel towards each other – and when those feelings take a turn for the worst.

Hard times

Married couples have to make a real effort at sharing each other's lives. If it works they can make each other happy, but there will always be low points which they must face together. Sadly, some marriages experience more lows than highs.

"Strangely enough, I was glad when Mum and Dad finished. Ever since I was little it was clear to me that simply being in each other's company made them miserable. It was like living in a laughter-free zone."

Ewan (14)

I love you, I hate you!

"Mum and Dad have been divorced for years, but they still send each other cards and presents at Christmas and on birthdays."

Nancy (14)

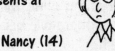

Love is a very powerful emotion. It can't be switched off like a light. In fact, it's possible to love someone and at the same time feel miserable being in a relationship with them. In the same way, some parents who have parted company can be left with happy memories and sometimes even no regrets.

Staying together for your sake

"My parents split up while I was in my first term at university. They travelled down to see me and explained they had waited until I'd left home before going ahead with the divorce. Although I put on a brave face, I didn't deal with the news very well. I felt guilty because they'd put on a pretence for so long just to keep me smiling."

Rob (19)

Even if it's clear that your parents don't love each other any more, it's still perfectly natural for you to want them to stay together. It gives you a feeling of security. Others may hope, often unrealistically, that things between their mum and dad will improve and return to the way they were in happier times.

To get a better view, step into your parents' shoes. If their marriage no longer makes them happy and nothing can be done to make it work again, pretending everything's fine will make them feel stuck in a rut. The atmosphere will become tense and there'll rarely be any fun.

When this happens, the sense of misery can rub off on you. That's why a separation or divorce is sometimes the only way for everyone to get out of that rut and to begin rebuilding their lives.

The end of the road

When do parents decide to separate? The timing differs in every case, but one thing's certain: the decision is never simple or quick to reach.

For a start it could be that only one parent wants to end the marriage. Perhaps one of them feels there is no future in living together any more, while the other is convinced that he or she can make things work again. If your parents no longer agree on a lot of everyday things, it may take them ages to accept that the marriage is over. Often it's considering how the split will affect you that makes the decision so agonising and traumatic.

It may also be that they will separate (in other words, live apart) and then wait years before actually divorcing and ending the marriage legally. A period of separation gives your parents the time and space in which to think, and to come to terms with living apart.

"My parents told me they were going to live apart because being together made them unhappy. But when Dad left home Mum cried for a week. Weird!"

Nicholas (15)

"Dad moved out for two days, then came home again. Everything was great between Mum and Dad for about a month, then they had another row and he left again. That time Dad didn't come back."

Joyce (15)

Splitting up, not giving up on you

When a marriage breaks down, parents sometimes feel they've failed their children. They also worry that you'll fret about losing the security of a stable home. As a result, after the split parents find themselves working harder than ever before to provide for you both emotionally and financially. Tight finances may mean that there'll be some cutbacks, but your parents will never shortchange your emotional well-being!

"When my parents separated I didn't think they cared about my feelings. Now I live with Mum, and Dad takes me out at weekends. They both make a real effort, and I know that splitting up was not an easy option for either of them."

George (17)

To help your mum and dad help you, try not to view the separation as an easy way out for them. In many ways splitting up is harder than staying together as it means such a big upheaval for the whole family. As a result, most couples with children will consider and try every possible way of making their marriage work.

The end of the world?

Make no mistake, witnessing your parents split can bring your mood crashing down for a long time. If you're feeling low, the best thing you can do is talk to people who have been through the experience of seeing their parents separate. They will tell you that with time you will get things in perspective and regain control of your life. The key, they say, is to look forward and believe that things will get better.

Looking forward doesn't mean pinning your hopes on a reunion between your mum and dad. It's easy to kid yourself that they'll soon make up, but this won't help you deal with the split and just makes it harder to accept things have changed. More importantly, it also distracts you from facing up to the future.

"One day I would wake up and think I'd got over my parents' separation, the next day I'd be so depressed I couldn't even face getting out of bed. I went on like this for months, but eventually my life returned to normal. Like puberty or a first kiss, I guess it's something you have to go through to understand what it's all about."

Neil (17)

Okay, it may seem like the end of the world, but let's start looking at the split as the beginning of a new life for you and for your family.

Finding a way forward

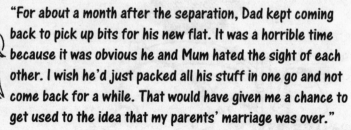

"For about a month after the separation, Dad kept coming back to pick up bits for his new flat. It was a horrible time because it was obvious he and Mum hated the sight of each other. I wish he'd just packed all his stuff in one go and not come back for a while. That would have given me a chance to get used to the idea that my parents' marriage was over."

Caroline (17)

Even though your parents might have separated without consulting you, now is the time you can really have your say.

You may be given the choice of which parent you would like to live with. Don't feel guilty about choosing between your mum or your dad. If your parents feel that you are responsible enough to choose, they must also be prepared to accept your decision.

Ask yourself whether living with your mum or your dad would make you feel most secure and happy. Don't forget that, whoever you choose, you will still get to see the other parent on a regular basis.

Of course, before you can make up your mind there are countless other questions to ask. If you're living with one parent, will they be any good at helping you with your homework? Will you still get to see both sets of grandparents? How will you get to school? Will the family home have to be sold? Will both parents have to work? Who's keeping the car? More

important, who's keeping the telly and the stereo?
And what about the cat!

Even though some of your questions might seem
trivial, every single one has to be asked. Make a list of
your questions – that way you won't forget anything!

Starting over

> "It took ages for me to get my head straight. When Dad
> left to live with another woman, the house suddenly
> seemed empty and Mum and I sort of rattled around
> in it."
>
> **Nicole (16)**

After the separation there will be changes to face
before your life settles down once more. It can be
difficult to keep your bearings. You may have to move
into a smaller house or change schools. Old routines
will be thrown out the window and you might not
know whether you're coming or going. Your parents
may start acting differently and sometimes strangely
as they come to terms with the split.

At times like this, you must reach out to steady
yourself. Find someone you trust, and talk to them
about what you're going through. It also means
asking the questions that you need answers to and, as
we'll see in the next chapter, making sense of the
strong emotional changes you'll be experiencing.

CHAPTER THREE

Your first feelings

Teenage life can be tough even when things are running smoothly. For a start there's school and the stress of exams. Then there's the fact that our bodies are developing at a crazy rate. This is down to our hormones which not only cause us to grow in jolts, but throw us into a whole new world of emotions. So when your parents separate, it can leave you exposed to strong feelings that you've never dealt with before and don't know how to handle.

What's more, your mum and dad may be so wrapped up in their own relationship problems that they find it hard to give you the support you need. Without the chance to talk your feelings through, a whole string of emotions can be wound up inside you. Before you know it, you're tied in knots.

"I just couldn't get my mind around the idea that my mum and dad didn't love each other any more. I even considered running away from home so that I wouldn't have to deal with the situation. Eventually I turned to my gran for help. She was the last person I thought would understand, but she did. She listened to my worries and explained what was happening."

Francis (15)

"Seeing your parents split up is a bit like sitting through a blockbuster film. You can be happy one minute, sad the next and have no idea how you'll feel later."

Elisa (14)

Your emotions don't simply line up to take turns in knocking you around like a novice on a judo mat! If one feeling takes you on then it tends to bring its mates along to give you a real kicking. This means that you might feel sad because your parents are separating and at the same time feel relieved that they're no longer shouting at one another and making everyone's home-life miserable.

The news might also make you feel numb, and yet something inside you says the split was bound to happen. You may even feel let down, despite the fact that your parents have told you they are separating for your sake. Whatever your situation, life immediately after the split can leave you feeling very mixed up inside.

"There comes a point when you realise there's nothing you can do to change things. It's only then that you find the strength to stand tall and face the future. You might feel mixed up inside about your mum and dad, but at least you're facing in the right direction while you deal with it."

David (16)

It's important not to bottle up your feelings, or assume you can handle your parents' separation alone. Without talking about your emotions, it's very hard to work out exactly what it is you're feeling.

Take the pressure off yourself by talking honestly with someone you trust. Your mum and dad will be expecting you to talk to them about what you're going through. Brothers or sisters will also share your feelings, and may be just as keen to open up. Use the opportunity. Talking is the first vital step towards coming to terms with what's happened. Eventually, you'll start to recognise each emotion and feel able and strong enough to tackle each one in turn.

When the news broke

Think of those moments in your past that will remain with you forever. There are the good things like a memorable holiday or your first kiss, but there are also those events that you wish had never happened.

Many people clearly remember the exact moment
that their parents came clean about what was
happening. The emotional impact is something
people rarely forget. But although they may look back
with sadness, it's also an experience that they learn to
value. Why? Because a great deal can be learned
about emotions and how to handle them.

Shock and disbelief

"I'll never forget that feeling when my dad
switched off the television and said that he
and Mum had something to tell me.
Afterwards, the silence was unbearable."
Howie (14)

"Before the split I used to think I knew my
parents inside out. Was I wrong!"
Peter (14)

"I didn't want to hear what they were
telling me."
Val (14)

Often, feelings of shock and disbelief are the first to
hit home. When they hit hard like this, you can panic.
Why? Because if you're not ready to deal with your
emotions, your first instinct could be to turn and
run. But before you even think about running away
from the situation, read on . . .

Dealing with it

Running away never solves any problems. In fact, turning your back will make the situation harder to handle. You may not accept what's happened for a while, but keep talking things through and you'll soon get a grip.

Sadness and grief

Grief counsellors often say that coping with divorce comes second only to dealing with a death in the family. When one parent leaves home it can feel as if he or she has gone for good. The trouble is you're unlikely to get the same sympathy and understanding from outsiders as you would if your mum or dad had died. You may not get time off school to deal with your feelings, and if your mates don't know the story, you feel obliged to keep going as if nothing's happened.

Dealing with it

A good cry can work wonders. Blubbing is a great way of releasing all those feelings that are giving you such a hard time. So drown those sorrows with tears, and if you're missing the parent who has left home then make sure you keep in contact. Call round if he or she has not moved far away. Alternatively, use the phone, write or if you've both got access to a computer then send an e-mail.

Once your mum and dad have established a visiting routine for you it will get easier, but for the time being make every effort to see them. Don't feel like you're pestering because the chances are that the absent parent will be missing you desperately too.

Other emotions

"Sometimes I had feelings about the split that I didn't think I ought to be having."

Ned (16)

Just as the circumstances for separation range from the big issues (Dad's drinking/Mum's affair) to the bizarre (his love of breeding gerbils/her dislike of moustaches) so your emotional reactions can be equally surprising. Yes, it's common to go into shock or to pretend it's not happening, cry and even mourn the end of your parents' marriage. But you're just as likely to feel emotions which take you by surprise; feelings that your friends may not expect or come close to understanding.

Anger and resentment

"For about a week after my parents told me they were splitting up, I was walking around like a time bomb ready to go off."

India (16)

Believe it or not, anger and resentment are actually common emotions to experience when parents split. Through your eyes it can seem as if your parents have dumped a load of problems on you at a time when you want to be free to concentrate all your efforts on chatting up people you fancy, having a laugh with your mates or just looking cool in the corridor. There's nothing wrong with seeing red, but be warned. The trouble with harbouring bitter feelings is that they can affect other areas of your life. For example, you may blame one parent for ending the marriage, but end up taking out your rage on a mate!

Dealing with it

Sometimes the best way to get anger and resentment under control is to release them. Shouting out your feelings is the most direct way, but the difficulty is finding someone who understands why you're cross and won't burst into tears when you take it out on them.

Alternatively, if you're feeling fit to explode, but don't want to frighten your friends, a spot of physical activity is a good way of venting pent up anger. Use any means at your disposal to let off steam, just as long as no one gets hurt by anything you say or do.

Guilt

> "I started thinking that if I hadn't been so moody
> with my parents over the last year then they might
> have stayed together."
>
> Jason (16)

Most parents go to great lengths to make sure their children aren't blaming themselves for the divorce. Even so, it's natural to feel that you may somehow be to blame. You convince yourself that if only you hadn't been such a noisy/scruffy/rude/pouting/lippy/sulky, consistently late and all-round disobedient son or daughter then maybe your mum and dad would still be together!

Dealing with it

So you think you've been behaving badly? Feel responsible for the break up of your parents' marriage? Think again. Parents actually expect teenagers to be difficult! Learning the hard way about your responsibilities in life is all part of the joys of growing up. Even if you're convinced that acting a little more considerately towards your parents may have kept them together, the chances are that something else would have eventually led them to separate.

Face facts – if your mum and dad were going to split up, there's nothing you could have done to stop them. Yes, teenagers can be a nightmare to live with, but they're rarely responsible for driving their parents apart.

Relief

> "When they told me they were splitting I was shocked, but it also felt like a dark cloud had lifted from over our house."
>
> Frankie (16)

If the split puts an end to all the arguments and upset at home, it's only natural to feel relieved. Perhaps violence has played a part in the marriage breaking down, in which case one parent leaving can make everyone feel relieved.

Dealing with it

Relief is often the last thing you'd expect to feel. Some teenagers think they should go into mourning, weep and wear black arm bands for months on end. But if in your heart you know that your mum and dad's separation was the only way forward for them and for you, then why shouldn't you be relieved?

Insecurity

> "When Mum left, I worried about what would happen to me and my brother. Dad was so cut up, he couldn't even talk to us for a little while."
>
> **Will (15)**

Often when one parent leaves home all sense of security walks out too. Perhaps you start to think that if one of them is capable of leaving the family home, perhaps the other will soon follow. Feeling like this can lead to a big dip in self-confidence that can easily get out of hand. When this happens, you need to look at the facts and bring reality back into your life!

Dealing with it

In many ways your mum and dad's decision to split will actually bring them both closer to you. Parents are acutely aware of how seriously the breakdown of their relationship affects their children. Having been preoccupied with sorting out their own problems, the separation will give them the breathing space to make themselves more available to you. Often this experience will bind you all together, especially if it has meant that you have all started talking openly and honestly with each other.

Your parents might be ending their marriage, but don't for a minute think that your parents are calling it quits with you.

If you've experienced some of these feelings just after your parents' split, and you're still in one piece, then pat yourself on the back. You've probably had a tough time and deserve to be congratulated!

CHAPTER FOUR

While the separation sets in

THE EMOTIONAL ROLLER-COASTER

"I'd go out with my mates and forget all about the fact that Dad had left home, but at the end of the day I'd have to go back and give Mum the support I thought she needed. It was hard work, but we got there in the end."

Felix (17)

A split between your parents sends everyone in the family reeling, but eventually you must find your feet and focus on moving on. Accepting that nothing will change things back to the way they were will help you to set your sights on the future. It's something you can plan for, influence and set out to enjoy. Things may never be the same again, but this doesn't mean your situation will get any worse.

Many find the prospect of feeling comfortable about their parents' separation a distant dream. Things will get better, however, but not overnight. Nobody ever wakes up and thinks, 'I'm over the blues. Time to get on with my life.'

The period between the decision to separate and the final divorce can often be a deeply unhappy and unsettling experience. During this time and for a long while afterwards there will be moments – even days – when you genuinely believe that your parents' separation has sunk in, but the next moment you will find yourself all worked up and upset again.

Eventually, the fact that your mum and dad live apart will seem more natural than if they were still under the same roof. Reaching that point can be hard work, so it's always worth being on your guard for some nasty feelings that may sneak up when you least expect them. Be prepared, and the problems won't have a chance to turn into a crisis.

Thinking things over and over and over

"For ages afterwards every thought I had seemed to be related to the divorce. If I was going riding, I'd remember how Dad used to take me to the stables in the car. When I heard a song on the radio, I imagined the lyrics were about Dad and Mum. Until I talked to my brother and found out that he was feeling the same way too, I thought I was going mad!"

Anthea (17)

Coming to terms with what's happened at home can be a long and bumpy ride – a real emotional roller-coaster. Time is an essential part of the healing process during which you need to work through your thoughts and let your feelings settle. The trouble is the longer you think about the situation, the more likely it is that your whole world will start to revolve around the separation!

While your thoughts are dominated by the divorce it's hard to feel entirely happy. It's as if there's a little black cloud hanging over your head that won't go away even when the Sun's shining. After a while, this constant gloom can bring you down.

Talking helps to ease the burden, but if the split happened a long time ago you may convince yourself that other people won't want to be bothered by your problems. This is often when the real trouble starts.

While you stay silent and brood, that little black cloud can get bigger, casting shadows over every aspect of your life. At times like this you don't need a weather forecaster to help you make sense of things, you just need to talk.

Loneliness and depression

"Nobody at school knew how I was feeling. They were aware that my dad had gone to live with another woman, but because I didn't raise the subject with them they never dared to ask me about it. Looking back, I wish I'd just come clean. After all, I'd done nothing wrong."

Joel (17)

For a long time after the split, the parent you live with may be preoccupied with their own thoughts and worries. They could also be working hard to make ends meet, and as a result find themselves unable to devote as much time to you as they would otherwise like.

Some find the break up involves moving to a new home and school, which means leaving old friends behind or even being separated from brothers and sisters. Combine this with the fact that you no longer see one parent every day and it's easy to see how lonely you may feel.

When you're hurting inside it's tempting to shut out the rest of the world, and if you haven't told your friends what's going on at home then they won't know how to help you. The only difference they're likely to notice is that you're running on a very short fuse!

Dealing with it

You should never feel ashamed about feeling depressed or unhappy. Don't hide your feelings, just keep talking them through. There's nothing wrong with shutting yourself in your bedroom to spend time on your own and think things over – it's all part of working out your feelings. But don't shut everyone out, from your room or from your thoughts. Open up and let friends and family come in and have a chat. Just make sure they knock first!

If you feel that you're bothering friends, or you think your parents have enough to deal with, then contact a counsellor or telephone helpline (see Chapter Ten). Even if that cloud above you has made things as dark as night, there are always people who will listen and lead you out into the light. It's just up to you to take their hand.

Stress

"I became very quick to lose my temper with friends, simply because Mum and Dad's divorce was looming. Just thinking about it put me on edge."

Camille (16)

Life is full of stresses. Without a bit of stress to keep us on our toes we'd all be that little bit less likely to take on bigger challenges and improve ourselves. It's when stress gets out of control that it becomes a damaging influence on our lives.

Stress is basically a combination of pressure, tension and anxiety. People claim they're stressed in many different situations. They may be revising hard for exams and start to worry about how well they're going to perform. Others get stressed when they carry a weight of responsibility on their shoulders and don't want to let themselves or anyone else down. It can arise in any situation where your thoughts and energy are focused on something that worries you. One of the biggest causes of stress among teenagers is dealing with the breakdown of their parents' marriage.

Witnessing your parents split up forces you to think about your future more than ever before. Without the familiar comfort of the family to fall back on, you stop taking things for granted and start to see life as a series of hurdles. If your parents have become wrapped up in their own problems then it's likely that you'll begin to take on more responsibility for yourself. Becoming less reliant on others can be a positive experience, however, as it teaches us the value of independence. Getting used to the idea of standing more on your own two feet though can give rise to a great deal of anxiety, wobbly moments and ultimately stress.

Dealing with it

You find yourself dwelling too long on the divorce then the simple answer is to find a relaxing way to distract your thoughts. Once you've stepped back from the problem, it's far easier to get things in perspective. It's a bit like staring for too long at a complicated maths question. You concentrate so hard that eventually nothing makes sense. But as soon as you go and make a cup of tea the answer springs to mind!

Forgetting it all for a moment

"After a while, I didn't want to hear anything more to do with divorce – I was sick of it! As a result, I'd try to block it out of my mind and pretend that it wasn't happening. Sometimes it felt good to forget about my problems. But then there were times when I knew I was just running away from reality."

Theo (15)

Everyone needs to take a break. From tea breaks to summer breaks, school breaks to ad breaks, we all need time out from our everyday lives in order to recharge our batteries and unwind.

In many ways a break is equally important when it comes to getting through your parents' separation. Every once in a while you need to get away from the situation, not just physically but mentally. Take up a sport, go out with friends and take a break from your worries.

Don't kid yourself that your problems will be gone by the time you get back, but if you feel refreshed on your return then they won't seem so scary or impossible to conquer.

Fantasies

"I used to have this daydream that I could go back in time and stop Mum and Dad from getting divorced. It was comforting for a while, but eventually I realised that

it was making it harder for me to accept that they were
never going to get back together again."

Martin (16)

It's only natural to want your parents to be reunited.
Sadly, in most cases the chances of a reconciliation
are pretty slim. But until your mum and dad have
been separated long enough for you to come to terms
with the situation, there will always be a dream in the
back of your mind that one day they'll patch things
up. It's a thought that is especially hard to shake if
one parent is unhappy about the divorce and the
other is determined to make the break. Over time
the dream will fade, but while it floats about in
your thoughts don't use it as a means of escaping
from reality.

Dealing with it

Rarely do dreams come true, so don't get your hopes
up. A reconciliation doesn't always mean that the
marital difficulties have come to an end, often it's just
the beginning of the same old story.

Setting up your parents

"I asked my parents to meet me for a coffee in town, but
'forgot' to tell each of them that the other was going to be
there. Looking back, that meeting was the most awkward I
have ever witnessed. They both stayed and were polite to
each other, but it was obvious they were doing it for my
sake. I felt such a fool!"

Raina (18)

There are many occasions when it's fun to play match-maker. Sending love notes on behalf of a friend can be a giggle. Asking someone out for a mate is fun too. Sometimes it works, sometimes it doesn't, but if it fails it's you who gets the blame.

When it comes to your mum and dad's relationship, you have to be aware that their decision to split is something that they've probably thought about long and hard. Separation isn't easy after years of marriage and living together. In many ways it's a harder step to take than staying together. It's unpleasant in the short term, but eventually everyone involved will be happier.

Dealing with it

In trying to bring your parents back together, all you're really doing is risking further misery for

everyone. Besides, if your mum and dad have decided to separate then really there is nothing you can do to change the situation. It may make you feel helpless, but you have to let go and accept what's happened.

A brighter way of looking at things is to set about strengthening your own relationship with both parents. Now that your parents are living apart and things are settling down, all the time they spent dealing with the problems in their marriage can now be devoted to you!

Wobbly moments

"I still sometimes wake up in the morning and forget that my parents don't live together any more."

Yvonne (15)

When anyone sets out on a new venture, there will be wobbly moments until everything settles down. Nobody can just pick up a guitar and expect to play an amazing solo (unless they're just pretending in front of the mirror). In the same way, not many people can claim they were pulling wheelies on the first day they learned to ride a bike.

As for coming to terms with your parents' separation, nobody expects you to shrug off the news and carry on as if nothing has happened. You need to grieve and talk about your feelings – it's the only way forward. But just as a professional guitarist will sometimes play the odd duff note, you may also hit an emotional time a long while after the split.

Blaming everything on the split

"Once at school I got into a fight with this lad about a girl we both fancied, and as a result I was hauled in front of the headmaster. He let me off because he knew I had 'family problems'. Obviously I was upset over Mum and Dad getting divorced, but I have to say that the fight had absolutely nothing to do with what was happening at home!"

Dean (18)

We all have bad days. Often we wake up with a frown and nothing will bring a smile to our faces. That's why it's important not to think that every emotion, feeling or low mark at school is in some way linked to the split.

You may not be at your best while you're dealing with things at home, but providing everyone around you knows your situation then you can expect some tolerance and understanding. Just don't overstep the mark and blame all your problems on the separation or divorce. Perhaps you're a terrible dancer, but claiming that this is due to trouble at home is a little hard to swallow!

Focusing on you

"Just after the split my aunt started taking me ice-skating. Not only was I good at it, but it gave me something to do."

Maxine (15)

"When I'm down about not seeing Dad I go to my room and paint."

Belinda (16)

"I can go for days feeling fairly normal, then I go through a bad patch when I can't stop thinking about Mum. To make myself feel better I go for a short walk. I usually end up meeting someone I know and having a chat. Sometimes I mention that I'm worried about Mum, but at other times the gossip's so good that I forget why I went for a walk in the first place!"

Brooke (17)

When the emotional wobbles hit, one way of getting your balance back is to concentrate on things, like a hobby or sport, that aren't connected with your parents or the separation.

When you make the effort to devote some time to yourself, it's a bit like riding a bike without stabilisers for the first time – you only have yourself to rely on. But go ahead, it will be worth it!

Learning from the experience

"When my parents divorced I vowed that if I ever married I'd never put my own kids through the same hell. Unfortunately, things didn't work out with my wife, so when we separated I made sure that my daughter felt able to talk to me about her feelings."

Jeff (38)

Separation or divorce are not something you will forget. Nor, for that matter should you try to cast them from your mind or pretend they never happened. The fact that your mum and dad have gone their separate ways will influence your life in many ways, both practically and emotionally, and it's up to you to recognise the positive lessons that are there to be learned.

New relationship skills

"After all we went through when Dad went to live with another woman, I found I could tell Mum that I loved her without feeling completely stupid or soppy. I definitely think the experience made me emotionally much stronger."

Reece (18)

Divorce can make some people take a close look at the way they relate to other people. At some stage during and after the separation of their parents, they find it helps to open up about their feelings to someone they trust. Talking about emotions like love, anger, embarrassment and fear takes a lot of guts. It can show a maturity in character that other teenagers may take years to equal.

Although it might not seem a valuable lesson at the time, witnessing your parents' marriage break up reveals a great deal about the downside of love. It's an unpleasant reality, but then not all romances work out as perfectly as they do in the movies.

Many teenagers whose parents have split are far more cautious about throwing themselves into relationships as they've seen what can happen when things go wrong. It has to be said, however, that there are some who feel badly let down by their parents, and as a reaction set out to find love elsewhere. Jumping into such relationships rarely brings them the security and happiness they seek.

There's nothing essentially wrong with getting involved with someone while your parents break up, it's just that you have to be honest about what it is that you're seeking from the romance, and how much you can contribute to the relationship while your family is undergoing such a difficult period.

New responsibilities

"Since Dad left I certainly feel I have to pull my weight around the house a lot more. I don't mind though, as it wouldn't be fair to let Mum do everything!"

Sheena (16)

Many people will tell you that it's easier dealing with your parents' divorce when you're a teenager than it would be if you were younger. You might think otherwise right now, and maybe argue that ignorance is bliss. But anyone with younger brothers or sisters will have seen how much harder it was for them to understand what was happening.

The harsh reality might be deeply unpleasant, but in being up-front and honest about the situation at least your parents have treated you like a young adult. You may have felt that the whole episode has aged you beyond your years, burdening you with responsibilities you might have otherwise avoided, but look at it another way – at least you'll be better prepared for anything else that life chooses to throw at you in the future!

CHAPTER FIVE

Life outside the family

"At the same time as my parents were splitting up I was really into going to my judo club. My teacher knew what was going on at home, and every time I turned up at a lesson he pretended I was some raging animal ready to take out my family hassles on the rest of the class. He was only clowning around but he always made me laugh."

Ali (16)

If you're thinking about the issue constantly, it's easy to let your parents' divorce become the focus of your world. Some people even find that their dreams begin to involve weird stuff about the separation! But waking up in the morning in a cold sweat and divorce on your mind is no good for anyone.

I'm off! See you later....

So before it goes this far, it's important to remember that you have a life outside the family.

Keep things in perspective. Just because your parents are separating, it doesn't mean the whole world is going to end. Whatever happens between your mum and dad, you'll always have your friends and outside interests. You may even suddenly find – much to your own surprise – that school is a great place. It lets you get away from all the home hassles for a while!

Stepping out while they split up

"Even when things were quiet at home, just being there was a constant reminder of all the arguments and slanging matches that had happened under that roof. I spent a lot of time going out with my mates, but at the end of the day I always went home. It was good to get away for a bit, but I knew there was no point in completely turning my back on the fact that my parents were splitting up."

Tina (16)

In our teens pressure swirls out from many areas of our lives. There's school, for starters, with its constant round of homework, revision and exams. Meanwhile your bodies are causing you grief by changing as fast as fashion. As a result it's easy to feel a bit insecure. To top it all, your hormones go crazy.

All these pressures can come together to form a whirlwind of confusion, anxiety and stress. So, when your mum and dad separate or divorce, it can be enough to send you mad with worry! But hang on in there! When the going gets rough at home, there are plenty of people you can turn to who can help you smooth out your worries.

Is anyone out there?

"I didn't like to admit that my mum and dad were splitting up. I was embarrassed about the situation, and I didn't think anyone would understand why I felt like this. What was weird was the fact that a friend of mine was going through exactly the same situation with his parents, but he hadn't told anyone either!"

Chester (16)

Many people see their parents' divorce as being unique – something that nobody else has ever experienced. In this frame of mind you can convince yourself that no one will be able to identify or understand how you feel, or worse still want to listen to what you've got to say!

As a result, you wander about with a stiff upper lip and pretend everything's cool. Even though your parents may be actively encouraging you to talk about your feelings, when it comes to opening up to anyone outside your immediate family – mum's the word!

If you do this you are ignoring the fact that there are thousands of people who have witnessed their parents' divorce. They've been there, seen it, done it and have come out in one piece. And it's not just friends who can help, there are other people who are aware of what's going on and who are more than willing to lend their support. It's just a question of knowing who those people are.

What families are for

"My aunt was really good to me when my parents split up. She took me out a lot when Dad was dealing with the fact that Mum had left. It was great to open up to her, but she was also aware that sometimes I didn't want to talk. Often I just wanted to get out for a while and put my worries to one side!"

Beth (15)

Families are a funny bunch. If everything's fine on the home front it's easy to forget how much they mean to us. When you're told that Auntie Anne and Uncle Jim are coming to stay, you groan and kiss goodbye to a weekend of lounging about in front of the telly. But if there's trouble at home, and your parents' marriage is in difficulty, you'll often find that the Auntie Annes and Uncle Jims of this world are the first to pitch in and help.

Sometimes they are aware of what's going on between your mum and dad even before you are. This is because when things start to go wrong, the first people your mum and dad are likely to talk to are their parents, brothers or sisters.

So don't shut out your family and sit in your room on your own feeling depressed. Leave your door open and let your family come in. They will take your mind off the split, they will take you out and they will be only too ready to listen.

If you have brothers or sisters, then it's good to talk to them as well. They are experiencing exactly the same feelings as you, and sharing your problems often helps to put them in perspective.

You're a mate, can I tell you something?

"My best friend was the first person I turned to when my parents split. Right from the start, she was brilliant about it. She listened when I wanted to talk, but didn't treat me like I was some kind of victim! I think it's the fear of feeling different to everyone else that actually stops some people admitting that their parents are divorcing."

Karen (16)

Many of us find it hard to express our true feelings. When we really fancy someone, for example, it takes courage to simply step up and ask them out. We're scared of being turned down and losing face. We may be mad about this person, but we're not mad on being honest about our emotions in case we end up being rejected. It's because we don't want to stand out in this way that most of us find it easier to put a stopper on our feelings. In the end, however, the signs always show. Look at what happens when someone mentions the name of the person we fancy – we turn bright red!

The trouble with bottling up your emotions about one issue is that it can have a negative effect on other areas of your life. Although it is nothing to be embarrassed about, it's only natural not to want to broadcast the news from the rooftops. The thing is, if you don't let anyone know what's going on, people will soon wonder why you're so tetchy when asked what's on your mind!

No matter how you go about dealing with the separation, it's important to let someone outside the family know what's happening. You may not want to talk about it in great detail, and that's fine. Just making a friend aware of the situation means they will be more understanding and better prepared to help when you do feel like getting things off your chest.

Sob stories, and how to stay dry-eyed

"I didn't find it too hard when I first told my best mate about Dad leaving home. It helped that we've known each other for ages and always talked about our feelings. But then I made the mistake of telling a few mates at school. As I was speaking, I remember suddenly becoming aware that the whole class was listening to me. It was awful. I couldn't get out of the room quickly enough!"

Francesca (15)

The prospect of breaking the news might seem daunting, but you really don't have to hold a press conference! The first time you speak up, confide in someone you trust like a boyfriend, a girlfriend or a close mate. Don't worry if your lower lip begins to tremble when you start to speak. In coming clean to someone who really cares for you, he or she can provide a shoulder to cry on if that's what you need.

Friends can be an important lifeline – don't pass them by. Play it right and you can rely on them to take your mind off things and to keep your life on track. Just because your parents are divorcing it doesn't mean that you can't go out and have a laugh with your mates every now and then! What's more, if you prefer not to go through the story over and over again, a good mate can explain to others why you may need a bit of space!

Opening up

> "Sometimes there are things you can talk about with your mates that you'd never dream of mentioning to your parents."
>
> Charles (14)

During a separation, many teenagers find that their parents are suddenly on their backs urging them to talk about their feelings. If you stay silent on the subject, your parents will assume the worst. What your parents may find hard to understand, however, is that you do not feel comfortable opening up to them on a subject as sensitive as divorce. It means talking on an intimate basis – something you may have never done with the two people you have lived with all your life.

Often, it's just easier to talk things over with someone who isn't directly involved — a friend, a relative, or even a teacher. There's no reason to feel any sense of guilt if you do find that you'd prefer to confide in someone outside the family. Just so long as your parents know that you can open up to someone, they'll rest easier.

Coping with school

"Soon after Dad left, my mum phoned my form
teacher to let her know what had happened. At first I
was really angry as I felt that it had nothing to do
with school. But in the end, I realised it was the right
thing to do because I found it hard to concentrate on
school stuff. It also meant that I didn't get hassled
by the teachers!"

Heidi (15)

When there's trouble between your parents, school can become a haven. Sadly, there are also times when it can be hell. If there's nothing but grief at home, some teenagers suddenly find that they can't wait to get through the school gates each morning. As a way of getting away from all their domestic hassles, they positively throw themselves into the classroom! Providing they're not completely blanking out what's going on at home, then school provides a sanctuary.

There are also times when home hassles have the opposite effect on school life. For example, if your evenings are spent trying to do homework while your parents argue in the next room, it can sap your concentration and leave you emotionally drained. Let's face it, while you're riding that emotional roller-coaster ride the last thing you'll want to sit through is a geography lesson about oxbow lakes!

It's not uncommon when you're troubled by changing family circumstances to become withdrawn or even aggressive when asked why you're acting oddly. If this is happening to you, then it's essential that you make sure that your teachers are aware of your home situation. Teachers are in the business of helping you tackle tough problems and they will be sympathetic towards your plight.

Putting your teachers in the picture also means that you will get to see them as individuals who are actively interested in your well-being, and not just as people who dish out homework and detention.

Standing out from the crowd . . . not!

"The day after my mum and dad split up I thought
everyone at school was looking at me! None of my
mates knew anything about what had happened, but
you get this horrible feeling that everything's changed
around you."

René (16)

Dealing with your parents' divorce will nearly always
bring out strong feelings. Some of these emotions you
may not have experienced before or talked about with
friends or family. What's more, many teenagers feel as
if somehow their parents have failed them by
separating. This in turn makes them feel too ashamed
or embarrassed to mention it to anyone outside the
family. What can follow is shyness and even an
unwillingness to take an active role in class. If you've
had to move house and swap schools, then this
feeling can take over! It's only when you open up that
you discover you're not alone.

Feelings of loneliness or of being different to others
are often strongest just after your parents have
announced their separation, and when the divorce is
granted. This is because it takes time to adjust to the
family changes and feel settled once again. But
despite everything, you're still the same person in the
eyes of your mates. Even if you've had to move
schools, it's your personality that counts, not the story
of your parents' divorce.

Work wobbles

"Every now and then I'd find my thoughts flying back to the divorce. Once, when I was in goal for the school football team, my mind was miles away. I was thinking about my dad's new place. It was only when the ball whistled over my head that I snapped out of it!"

Bryn (15)

Unless you're a racing driver or a heart surgeon, it's almost impossible to concentrate on something 100 per cent of the time. It doesn't matter how committed you are to the task at hand, there will always be thoughts from other aspects of your life that come into your mind. When your mum and dad split up, however, this issue can take over and push all other thoughts (even the happy ones) aside. That's why it's not a good idea to get behind the wheel of a Formula One racing car or to perform major surgery if your parents have just divorced!

Time, of course, is the great healer here. As you adapt to the changing situation at home, your parents' separation or divorce will become a part of your past. This doesn't mean that it will no longer influence your life. As we've seen, it's important to watch out for the wobbly moments – those sudden plunges into black thoughts when you least expect them, and often when you thought the worst was over!

Sometimes the smallest thing can make you feel as numb as you did on the day your mum and dad first admitted their marriage was over. An anniversary, for example, or a celebrity divorce in the news can easily bring memories of the past flooding back. Moments like this are easier to deal with at home, especially when one or both parents are watching out for emotional stumbles. But if you're at school or college it's a different matter, especially if you've told everyone that you're sorted.

If a wobbly moment affects your concentration and turns into a work wobble, then you must be honest about it with your teachers. Like your parents, they'll be watching out for you long after the divorce has happened. Sometimes, however, it's up to you to remind them.

I wanted to take it out on the world

"Sometimes I feel so angry about what has happened. You think everything in life's turned against you, but all you end up doing is punishing yourself."

Archie (16)

"Stuff that never used to bother me in the past suddenly really bugged me. My friends thought I was losing it one day when I went mad at this guy for moving my PE kit!"

Edward (15)

All of us were cute once. When we were ankle-high there was little wrong we could do in the eyes of our parents. Then, we grew up and started to have thoughts, feelings and desires of our own. On hitting our teens we won't do anything for our parents without first answering back or kicking up a fuss, but still they love us. They know what it's like to be a teenager – they were once your age too – and they know that you'll wise up just as they did.

All parents know that the best thing they can provide is a secure environment in which their children can learn from their own mistakes. But then when your parents go and split up, it's enough to make you want to scream!

It may seem out of character to others, but this sense of frustration and anger is perfectly natural. Expressing it is an important part of coming to terms with what's happened. In some cases, however, it's crucial not to let your emotions become bitter.

There's nothing to be gained from getting nasty and spiteful, and doing things just to get back at your parents. Running a ring through your nose or running away from home will ultimately hurt only one person and that's you!

Rebel with a cause

"I don't think I was a very nice person just after Dad left home. I resented him for leaving, and took it out on my boyfriend. Then, when my boyfriend dumped me I fell in with a really bad crowd and started bunking school to hang around with them. I knew it

*upset Mum, but I guess it was my way of getting back at her
for everything that had happened!"*

Jenny (17)

In many ways rebelling against your parents is easier
than sitting down with them and talking about your
feelings. This is because rebelling lets you run away
from problems, rather than facing up to them. Being
a trouble-maker can make life difficult for your mum
and dad, but really it's just the idea of punishing them
that appeals. Seeing them hurt by your negative
behaviour will only bring on feelings of guilt in you.

Everyone rebels to some extent during their teens.
Dyeing your hair red for example, saves you having to
walk around saying 'I'm an individual. Notice me!'.
However, it's really not so cool when you decide to
rebel as a way of testing how far you can push
your parents.

Most teens who do go down this road don't actually
enjoy what they're doing. Being the cause of misery
and upset isn't something to be particularly proud of.
That's why, after your parents split, it's important to
deal with any anger before it starts to fester.

Sorted stress-relievers

*"I play guitar in a band with some friends. Normally we
play pretty ambient stuff but after my parents split the
others in the band complained that I was increasing the
tempo, raising the volume and rocking out! "*

Glen (15)

Anger, when dealt with sensibly and calmly, can be a positive emotion and, in the right hands, it's an energy that can be used for creative purposes. The only problem is how to express your anger in a constructive, not destructive way.

A physical response may be the first thing that springs to mind, but it's not a good idea to go round punching anyone who mentions your parents' problems. What you need is a less scary way of letting off steam – one that isn't going to get you into trouble.

Every time you sense the pressure mounting inside, use one of the following sorted stress relievers to help

you calm down and get it out of your system.

Jogging

This helps burn the energy that has made you feel fit to burst. It's certainly harder to get worked up when you've worked out, so any sport will help you keep calm.

Writing

Believe it or not, you can set your anger down on paper by writing about how you feel. Start off by writing, 'I am angry because . . .' and see where your pen takes you. Whatever works, do it. A poem, lyrics, even voodoo-style doodles will do the trick. And you never know, one day when you're famous your doodles might fetch a fortune.

Talking

Yup, it's the oldest way of channelling those negative feelings, but it works wonders. Make sure you talk your anger through with someone who knows what you're experiencing and who won't be upset by anything outrageous you may say!

It's fine if you feel as mad as hell over what's happened between your parents. Just find a way of getting things off your chest without hurting other people or yourself.

CHAPTER SIX

Dealing with divorce

"I'd only just started to accept that my dad had moved out when Mum started talking about divorce. When a friend at school said they'd have to go to court I was worried out of my mind! I thought Mum wanted to punish Dad because he didn't want to be married to her any more!"

Caroline (16)

Once your parents have separated, then at some point they will probably consider getting a divorce. Basically this means that their marriage will be legally ended.

GUILTY!

There are many different reasons for making the move from separation to divorce. Your mum or your dad may want to remarry, while in other cases a divorce is the only way to settle financial disagreements or a feud over which parent gets the infinite pleasure of looking after his or her treasured teenage son or daughter (which is, of course, a joy and an honour!).

Parents who separate without divorcing can make their own arrangements for your care and support. Once they've decided on divorce, however, then the courts must be consulted. When people talk about divorce and the law, it's easy to picture your parents standing in the dock before some frowning judge in a dusty white wig! But before you jump to conclusions, let's take a look at the facts:

- Divorce does not mean any of your family have committed a crime.
- Nobody will be punished because a marriage has ended.

The whole legal process positively encourages parents to settle any differences they have without battling it out in a courtroom. Only when your parents really can't agree on major issues will a court make a decision on their behalf. Even if this does happen, remember that your parents are not crooks and they won't be treated as such. The role of the divorce court is to simply make sure that everybody – including you! – is treated in the fairest possible way.

Even if your parents can't agree on anything (apart perhaps from wanting a divorce) it's important for you to understand that both of them will have your interest at heart. It's just they each have a different opinion of how best to go their separate ways without causing too much upset in your life.

The final step

> *"During their divorce Mum made quite a few phone calls to her solicitor. She also had to go for a couple of meetings. One of these meetings involved Dad, and it was really hard on her because they didn't get on. I didn't have much to do with the whole thing as my parents had always agreed that I should stay living with Mum, which suited me. Besides I had other things on my mind, like this really cute boy who'd just moved into our street!"*
>
> Nicole (16)

Sometimes parents can't wait to get divorced, while others may leave it for years before making the split official. Both parents don't necessarily have to agree on getting a divorce before legal proceedings can go ahead, though often it cuts out a lot of grief if they can see eye-to-eye.

When the divorce procedure starts you may feel unhappy emotions being churned up all over again. This is because a divorce is like the full stop at the end of a relationship. You have to accept that there is now no chance of your parents getting back together again as husband and wife. For this reason it's okay to feel blue, but there's no need to go pale with fright. You may have to talk to someone official about which parent you would be most content to live with, but no-one will be led off in handcuffs!

When will it happen and where?

"The day my parents' divorce came through, it suddenly struck me that they'd never get back together. Ever since I moved out with Mum, I guess I'd secretly believed that eventually she would make up with Dad. On the bright side, the divorce did encourage me to get on with my own life!"

Elisa (14)

To get divorced one parent must file a petition at the County Court. This doesn't mean that one parent knocks on the neighbour's doors gathering signatures against the other! Basically this petition is just a form that your mum or dad fills in that briefly spells out the grounds for the divorce.

As the law stands, one or both of your parents must prove that their marriage has 'irretrievably' broken down. This means that nothing can be done to keep them together as husband and wife. Short of waving a winning lottery ticket in front of their noses and seeing whether they miraculously kiss and make up, there are basically five ways to establish that nothing can be done to save the marriage:

1. If both parents have lived apart from each other for at least two years, and both of them want the divorce.
2. If they've been separated for five years, even though one parent doesn't want to get divorced.
3. If one parent has deserted the other for at least two years.

4. If one parent has behaved unreasonably towards the other (through physical abuse, for example, or because of a problem with alcohol or other drugs, or gambling).

5. If one parent has committed adultery. (This means that one parent has had a sexual relationship with someone else.)

If one of the first two ways of proving that the marriage is finished cannot be satisfied, then either the husband or wife has to convince a court that the other was 'at fault'. However, many people argue that asking one of them to stand up and take the blame for a failed marriage is a bit like punishing a football team for losing a match even though they tried very hard to win. These people say the law doesn't recognise that sometimes marriages just don't work out, no matter how much each partner has tried to steer things back on course.

The question of fault and how to prove it is a much-debated subject, and changes to the way divorce works are often considered by the powers that be. Eventually, this could mean couples will no longer have to prove one of them was responsible for the marriage breaking down. Also, before any marriage is officially ended, parents could be given a longer period of time to think about what the divorce will mean for everyone involved. During that time they may try to settle any major differences or even change their minds about the whole thing!

Whatever happens, don't be under any illusion that a

cooling off period would guarantee that your parents get back together. Time may be a great healer but it can't perform miracles!

It's important to face up to the fact that once the judge is totally satisfied that your parents can't be reconciled, then the divorce will probably be granted. Even so, when children are involved the court will make absolutely sure divorce is the best step forwards. To do this they must hear the opinion of everyone involved, including you.

Talk now!

"My parents took about three years after the separation before they got round to getting divorced. There was no hurry as my grandpa had made them sit down together when they first split up so they could sort out things like who I'd be living with. Back then my mum thought he was interfering, but now she keeps telling me how much energy, time and money Grandpa had saved them!"

Andrew (15)

Once a petition has been made for a divorce, your parents will be given every opportunity to sort out their affairs without standing before a judge. In some districts they may be referred to the court welfare service, or to a local out-of-court service that can offer a course of mediation.

Mediation allows your mum and dad to take part in sessions with an outsider. This outsider is a cross between a counsellor and a referee (without a whistle!). The idea is that your parents will be encouraged to keep talking calmly so they can tackle their differences and come up with a plan for the future that both of them accept.

The most important question that is discussed is your welfare. It's vital that both parents establish how much each will contribute to your upkeep. This is known as maintenance. In special cases where, for example, a lump sum of money is in question, a maintenance application will be made directly to the court. Usually, however, an assessment will be made by the Child Support Agency (CSA). This is an organisation that looks at your individual situation, ignores any personal pleas by you for a new pair of trainers, and works out who pays how much and when!

If your mum and dad can fairly and reasonably agree on every issue surrounding the divorce, and you're quite happy with the outcome, then the whole process can be relatively hassle-free. Neither of your parents even need to be present at the court hearing, and the divorce settlement can largely be dealt with by post. But even in the most clear-cut cases, there are nearly always one or two murky areas that have to be sorted.

Who keeps the cactus? Who gets the kids?

"My mum and dad didn't fall out about me or my brother. They agreed on who should have the car, and how much Dad would pay to Mum to help her look after us. They only fell out about one thing, our dog, and because of it they nearly ended up in court!"

Obi (15)

In all their years of marriage, your mum and dad will have acquired many things together, and they also will have shared the responsibility for bringing up you, their little treasure. And among all their shared possessions (excluding perhaps the odd item) you'd be hard pressed to find anything in your house that they both hold dear to their hearts in equal measure.

Now that your parents have separated, just imagine what would happen if a divorce court didn't exist to help them settle their differences and sort out the contents of the house. How else could they establish the best way forward for themselves and for their children? Without some kind of official way of sorting things out and sharing everything fairly, the situation between them could easily get out of hand.

There is a story that often does the rounds about how one man thought better of going to the court to settle his marriage dispute and instead tried to saw his house in two! And as for you, it's not as if each parent could take one of your arms and tug until one of them let go!

How are things decided?

"Mum and Dad divided up everything fairly, apart from the armchair, which they tossed a coin for!"

Jay (14)

For your mum and dad to divide things satisfactorily really depends on the circumstances of their divorce and how well they still get on.

Obviously it's hard for them to sort everything fairly if one of them feels they've been badly treated by the other. But when there are children to consider it's likely that they'll concede a few things if it means keeping upset to a minimum.

Divorce doesn't really mean that absolutely everything will be split 50/50. It just wouldn't be practical for your dad to take things like one speaker from the stereo while your mum kept the other. Most of the time they will compromise. Your dad gets the stereo, for example, providing your mum has the car that she needs for work. In every case, however, there's one thing that will take a great deal of careful thought and consideration, and that's the question of which parent you'll be living with and where your home will be.

Where do I fit in?

"I felt like a traitor when I said that I wanted to live with Dad. Although I felt bad at the time, it wasn't as if I was saying that I loved one parent more than the other. The way I look at it, my parents got me into that situation by splitting up in the first place. I'm just glad they let me have my say."

Simon (16)

After the separation it may not be practical, or even financially possible, for you and one parent to carry on living in the family home. If your mum and dad can't agree whether one of them should stay in the house, or if instead it should be sold and the proceeds split, then the court may have to make the decision.

If you have to move, the judge hearing the case will make sure that it's really in your best interest to do so. Where possible, the court will also make sure that you are not separated from any brothers or sisters.

Providing you were born within your parents' marriage, both your mum and dad have what's called parental responsibility for you. This means that whatever living arrangements you sort out, they will both have an equal say in your welfare.

In practice, of course, it's the parent you live with who has the greatest influence on your day-to-day affairs. But just because one of your parents isn't around to ban you getting your nose pierced, that parent is still expected to contribute financially to your upkeep while you're in full-time education.

It's your welfare that is most important to them both, no matter which parent you're living with. Whether it's your mum or your dad who gets to deal with your septic nostril and other day-to-day disasters, it's not so much what they personally want as what will be right for you!

Speaking out

"I was relieved that Mum kept asking me what I wanted after the divorce. It meant I could get things off my chest and even talk to her about the possibility of me living with Dad. The only trouble was that every time I saw my father he always avoided the subject. When I finally asked about living with him, it turned out that he had just assumed I wanted to stay with Mum!"

Fiona (14)

As an individual, with thoughts, opinions and feelings of your own, you should be consulted at some stage about which parent you think it would be best for you to live with. In some cases, however, your wish may not be granted because it's just not practical. Here are some examples:

• The parent you want to stay with has to work away from home for long periods. As a result, he or she may not be at home much to look after you.

• One parent has been behaving badly towards the rest of the family. In this case it may be clear that living with him or her would not be sensible. For example, if one parent had problems relating to alcohol or violence, and living with him or her would put you at risk of harm, then the court would almost certainly award responsibility to the other parent.

If either your mum or dad has always stayed at home

to look after you, however, then it's likely that the court will decide to keep things as they are. Whatever the outcome, both parents will still love you equally – no judge or court can influence that. Also, the absent parent will still be expected to have a say in your welfare, see you on a regular basis and also make financial contributions to keep you fed and clothed.

Living with one parent might mean money's tight, but no-one will expect you to start cleaning chimneys for a living just yet!

Before any decision can be made about which parent you'll live with, the court may ask for a report to be made. This isn't like a school report – you can't flunk it like you can maths or history. It's just a way of making sure that you haven't been pressured into choosing who you'll be living with, and that the decision is something that will work for all of you.

Heads it's Dad, tails it's Mum

"It's hard being put in the position where you have to say something that one parent isn't going to want to hear. What you have to remember is that you're dealing with your future. In my case Dad reckoned it was best that I lived with him because Mum had fallen in love with someone else. But as far as I was concerned, Mum had brought me up and she was the one I turned to whenever I had a problem. Why would a divorce change that?"

Anthea (17)

Given the choice, how do you go about deciding which parent would be best for you to live with? Obviously you have to be sensible about this, and not choose one simply because he or she has a bigger telly than the other, or lets you stay up later!

There are loads of things to consider, like where your mum or dad intends to live and whether this would involve a change of school. Don't feel disloyal while you're thinking things over. If you can it's good to sit down with both parents and discuss things with them. After all, it could be that your idea of life with one of them may not be what he or she had in mind.

For example, your mum may seem like a better option because she's always stayed at home and sorted your meals for you and acted as unpaid taxi driver, but after the divorce she may have to find a full-time job just to keep food on the table.

Ask as many questions as you can and try not to be embarrassed about embarrassing your parents! If Dad has a new love in his life, for example, ask him if she will be living with him? He may turn as red as a beetroot in a sauna, but you have the right to know all the facts. Also try to find out how often you'll get to see the absent parent, and whether you can change your mind about the living arrangements if things don't work out as anticipated.

If your mum and dad have left it up to you to decide, steer clear of the sympathy vote. The divorce may have affected one parent badly, and you may feel that by staying with that parent you'll stop his or her life from going down the tubes, but would this really make you happy? Would it be the best way forward for everyone concerned?

It's these kinds of things that a welfare officer may ask you if the court has asked for a welfare report. This will nearly always happen when your parents can't agree about who you'll be living with.

Sure, welfare officers have a scary teacher-type title, but you'll find they're really good people. They'll come and talk to you about things on a one-to-one basis, and then maybe ask you and your parents to come and have a chat together. This doesn't happen in the courtroom, but usually in a small room in the same building. No handcuffs or fingerprints, just coffee and biscuits.

Hey, judge!

> "Just before my parents' divorce hearing I found out that the judge wanted to speak to me. I thought that I'd done something wrong, but all he wanted to tell me was that my parents had said how mature I'd been about the whole thing! I smiled throughout our meeting, but I felt sick as a dog inside!"
>
> Jake (15)

Once the report has been presented to the court you may still be asked to appear at a hearing. Again, it's most likely to take place in a room next door to the court, but this time the judge will sit in and discuss things before finally making his or her decision.

In some instances the dispute is heard in court, but it's unlikely that you will say anything; the court welfare officer can speak on your behalf. All-in-all there's really nothing to panic about. Even if you do want to say your bit in court, just remember that nobody's on trial, and anything you say will not be used in evidence against you!

Decisions, decisions

"It was agreed that I'd go and stay with Dad every other weekend. At first I thought, 'Oh great – bang goes my social life,' but he's been brilliant. He makes a real effort to do things I enjoy."

Dad (16)

In cases where your parents agree on everything and you're happy enough with the big scheme of things, then the court may not need to make any decisions on your behalf. However, when there is a dispute over which parent you'll be living with or how often you can get to see the absent parent, then the judge will make an order.

An order is basically a kind of rule concerning your welfare that both parents agree to stick with until you've finished full-time education or reached the age of eighteen.

In England and Wales, the courts can make these decisions according to the Children's Act of 1989. In Scotland, this Act does not apply, but many aspects of the proceeding are similar.

Here are the main orders that may be decided:

Residence orders

When parents can't agree about which one of them you should live with, the court decides on their behalf. In a few cases, a joint residence order can be made. This means you would divide your time between living with your mum and your dad, but the court would have to be convinced that this arrangement will be in your best interests.

A residence order used to be called a 'care and control' order or 'custody', and in Northern Ireland these terms are still used in law. Because the change is fairly recent, however, you may find that friends whose parents are already divorced may use these words instead.

Contact orders

This is an order that is made when your parents can't agree on how much time you'll spend with the absent parent. However, once the residence order has been made, your mum and dad will often come to their own decision about how frequently you'll see the absent parent. As soon as this has been agreed by the judge, who will have asked for your opinion on the matter, then your parents must stick to it.

A contact order used to be called 'access', and a typical example might be staying alternate weekends with the absent parent, plus a week at Easter, summer and Christmas. Whatever the case, a contact order sets no limits on the number of times you phone, write, e-mail or even send smoke signals to the absent parent!

Specific issue order

It could be that your parents agree on all aspects of your welfare apart from one thing. For example, they might agree that living with your mum is best, and that you can meet up with your dad on three weekends a month. But when it comes to deciding which school you should go to, they might find it impossible to see eye-to-eye. When this happens, the judge steps in, has a chat with you to find out what you think, and makes the decision with a specific issue order.

There are two other main orders that the court can make. One is called prohibited steps. This order prevents one parent doing something that the other forbids – for example, moving you abroad.

The other order is called family assistance and is only required in exceptional circumstances when the parent you live with needs help, advice or assistance from someone outside the family.

Whatever the case, court orders can be made long after the divorce. If, for example, your mum and dad's circumstances change or if they cannot agree on an issue concerning you then an order can be made. Contrary to what you might think, the law can actually be quite flexible!

What difference will the divorce make?

"The day the letter came through saying my parents were officially divorced, Mum joked that she was young, free and single again. I wasn't so sure about the young bit, but I could tell she was looking forward to enjoying her life again!"

Jason (16)

Even if your parents are hugely relieved at getting the divorce, there's also a strong chance that they'll go through a period of sadness. This can seem confusing, especially if your mum and dad have given the impression that there's nothing they would rather own than a little piece of paper that says they're not married any more.

Why the mood swing? Well, divorce is certainly a milestone in anyone's life, but unlike your first kiss or having a surprise birthday party it's not something to look back on with any great sense of fondness. So if the parent you're living with becomes quiet and depressed, or starts acting differently just after the divorce, try to give them space and lots of understanding. Your parent has just come through a marriage that started off with high hopes but which has sadly come to an end. You can help by letting the parent know that he or she has your support for the future.

Now the divorce is over you can get back out into the real world. Just think about how much time you've given over to fretting about your parents' divorce. Every time you set eyes on your mum or dad, it would have been prominent in your mind. Life after divorce can take some getting used to, but at last you'll be able to talk to them about things that don't involve the dreaded 'D' word!

CHAPTER SEVEN
Torn in two

"The most difficult time for me came after my parents were divorced. The arguments stopped but instead of the peace and quiet I had hoped for, my mum kept turning to me whenever she had a problem. This meant I felt obliged to stay in most of the time until she'd got used to the idea of being single again. Worse still, my dad's social life was booming – he was always going out with his mates – while mine was in the pits!"

Tina (16)

Sometimes, the strain of witnessing your parents split can threaten to become too heavy to handle. Throughout the whole process of separation and divorce there'll be moments – even days – when you feel as though you've had enough, and all you really want to do is turn your back on it and walk away. There may even come a time when you'd like nothing more than the chance to divorce your mum and dad!

Even if there have been no squabbles or public dramas between your parents, any tension that exists is bound to rub off on you. Your mum and dad may do everything they can to make sure you don't suffer too badly from their decision to go their separate ways. For example, they might bend over backwards to ensure that you're happy with the new living arrangements and that you're not bottling up feelings you can't handle alone. Yet no matter how hard your parents try to keep things normal, there'll be no hiding from you the fact that they too are experiencing a big change in their lives. After years of living as a married couple, suddenly they're forced to adjust to living without each other.

If your mum and dad can remain on good terms throughout the divorce, then your day-to-day life may not change very much. In some cases, however, the break might bring to one or both parents a great sense of relief and freedom. As a reaction, one of them may plunge into a new lifestyle which, in your view, may be unsuitable or just plain embarrassing!

For other parents, the break up might be the last

thing he or she is prepared to handle alone. This puts pressure on you to stick around and pick up the pieces. Whatever the situation, watching your mum and dad adapt to their new lives can sometimes leave you surprised, shocked and often irritated.

Who's the grown-up here?

Just as your emotional world can go into a total spin when your parents part, your mum and dad will also experience a whirl of totally conflicting emotions. In seeking advice, help and support during this time, they'll often turn to you.

"After the divorce my mum started acting like a mate, always wanting to talk about this guy she fancied and even pinching my make-up! Once I told her to back off and give me some space, but afterwards I just felt sorry for her. In the end, I just had to accept that it was a phase she was going through."

Frankie (16)

If you find that your mum or dad are over-burdening you with their problems or invading your personal space while they find their feet, then you must speak up for yourself. It's great if your parents feel able to talk to you, but they mustn't forget that you have your own life to live and that you're not just the family agony aunt or uncle!

Until you say otherwise, they may not realise the pressure they're putting you under. If you feel uncomfortable talking to them about this, or find that the message doesn't seem to have got through, then talk to a relative or family friend who can have a word with your parents.

My parents are acting like kids!

"My parents behaved like spoiled children right through the divorce. Whenever they met Mum would just pout and refuse to look my dad in the eye. Once they fell out when my girlfriend was visiting me. Afterwards she made me swear that if we ever argued we'd be able to sort things out like adults!"

Nathan (15)

You know how it is when you fall out with a mate. In the heat of the moment it's easy to flare up or say something hurtful that goes nowhere towards sorting out the problems between you. The same can be said for some parents when their marriage breaks down. They would, of course, love to settle their differences calmly, but sometimes a situation arises where it's hard for them to control their emotions and stay cool. From an outsider's point of view, such as yours, their behaviour can seem foolish and at times downright childish.

Before you despair of your parents, try to accept that both of them will be under tremendous pressure to sort out their family affairs so that everyone can get on with their lives. Sure, they may say things that

they'll come to regret when they've got their sensible
heads screwed on. Just don't get sucked in before
they've had a chance to realise that they're acting like
overgrown kids.

If you feel strongly that one of them needs to be told
that he or she is behaving unreasonably, then just
make sure you approach that parent when he or she
is alone, calm and collected. Be aware that you're
bringing up a sensitive subject, one that could cause
further upset. Play your cards right and your parent
should see sense.

Steering clear

"When my parents divorced they both still wanted to know
what was going on in each other's lives. Sure enough it was
me, of course, who they tried to use to find out this
information. When I went round to Dad's, he'd always ask
'innocent' questions about Mum's boyfriend. Likewise, Mum
often tried to find out what was going on in Dad's love life.

In the end I just told them to start talking to each other again, as that was the only way they were going to find out anything."

Howie (14)

Even though your parents have stopped living together, it may take some time before they can actually do without each other. Having shared a great deal for so long, it's hard for them not to be just the teeniest bit curious about how their ex is getting on. To do this they need to find someone who knows them both well, someone who stays in regular contact and someone who won't mind being asked a few questions. Now, who could that be?

If you feel that one parent is leaning on you to reveal stuff about the other, just ask yourself why they need to know all this information. Often it's all fairly innocent. When your mum or dad are genuinely interested in knowing how the other is doing it'll be obvious to you. But if the questioning seems at all odd, or if they persist in asking you one specific question or encourage you to talk about something in particular, then make it plain that you're not playing their game. If it means so much to them, then they must find out for themselves by asking their former partner. By spilling the beans, especially before a divorce, you could be providing one parent with ammunition against the other. So stay safe by steering clear.

Playing parent ping-pong

"Seeing my mum without my dad was weird. What made things even harder was the fact that she'd gone to live miles away with this guy. Before the contact order was sorted, I spent most of my weekends travelling back and forth on the train because I didn't want to disappoint anyone!"

Kerry (15)

After a separation, you often find yourself doing a fair bit of flitting between parents. At times you can feel like some kind of ping-pong ball, bouncing back and forth from one home to another with no time to get your bearings at either end. Eventually you will settle down and get into a routine.

In fact, there are even advantages to living in two homes that only become clear when you actually try it out. But until you've got your head around the fact that your parents lead separate lives, and while they're still getting over the split, bouncing from one home to another will take a bit of getting used to.

In some cases it really can feel like a game, especially if one parent feels so resentful toward the other that he or she assumes you should feel the same way too.

Feeling under pressure to take sides or being used by one parent to score points against the other can be a deeply unsettling experience. That's why it's important to recognise when things are heading that way so that you can avoid getting involved.

• Don't let one parent make you feel that visiting the other is some kind of terrible ordeal that you have to endure, like being made to clean out the school toilets every other week!

• Don't hide your feelings if you miss the absent parent. If you haven't visited your mum or dad in a while, it's only natural to look forward to seeing her or him without feeling any sense of guilt.

• Don't allow one parent to constantly bad mouth the other in front of you. For example, if your mum makes out that your dad's a devil just remind her that it's her opinion and not yours. Her low opinion has been formed because of problems in her marriage and its breakdown, and not in your relationship with her or your father.

It has to be said that speaking out is hard if one parent steps over the mark or starts to sway your feelings in their favour, but if you can blow the whistle on any games before things get out of hand then eventually everyone will be a winner. For starters, it gives you a chance to concentrate on balancing life with two separate parents. Which begs the question . . .

Which house is home?

"Because Dad didn't live far away from Mum, it was agreed that I'd live alternate weeks with each parent. To begin with it was a novelty, but after a while it became a bit of a drag. It was hard to get settled when they each had different routines. In the end I realised that there were both advantages and disadvantages to living with either of them. Dad was a terrible cook, for one thing, but I had a bigger bedroom at his house."

Karen (16)

Whether you've had to move to a new place, or stayed put with one parent while the other packed their bags, at some stage you'll find yourself in the position where there's a chair for you around the table in two different homes. Even if you don't get to see one parent for a long period of time, when you do go to stay you'll probably be encouraged to treat his or her house as your own.

So how do you settle into life with two of everything? Is it hard adjusting to sleeping in two different beds? Do you ever wake up, forget you're in the 'other house' and wonder who changed the colour of the curtains while you were asleep? Like most things in life, change is something we can only get used to over time. Eventually, it will seem perfectly natural to have some of your CD collection stashed at your mum's and the rest at your dad's.

In the beginning, however, it may well feel like you're

leading two different lives. Much depends on how your time is divided. If you only stay with your dad on two weekends a month, for example, then there's not much point in shifting half your stuff to his home. In settling into two different homes you will have to work out what things you will need most in each one.

At the new place, it's also worth having a word with your mum or your dad about how you'd like to decorate your room. A lick of paint can help to make it feel like your own private space. What's more, hanging your favourite poster on the wall will put a familiar face in what may at first seem like strange surroundings. Give your new room the personal touch as soon as you get in there. Let's face it, you're not going to feel all tucked-up and cosy if you feel like you're sleeping in the spare room!

There are many reasons why you may favour one house over the other. For example, if your mum lives in the middle of nowhere, but your dad has a cool studio in the centre of town, then obviously there'll be attractions in kipping over at his place.

But putting aside the various attractions of each parent's home, the important thing to remember is that both your parents care for you in equal measure. Even if one of them is more laid back than the other about doing the washing-up or coming home at a certain time, try not to see these as sensible reasons for staying with one particular parent. Just accept that your mum and dad are individuals with their own standards, rules, routines and tastes. Now that they're divorced there's no problem if they want to lead different lifestyles. As for you, it's a chance to get the best out of both worlds!

Who loves you the most, sweetie?

"Both Mum and Dad were constantly trying to please me during the divorce. My dad would hold his temper if I stayed out late, and when I was with Mum she always cooked my favourite food. It sounds great, but to be honest I felt as if they were each trying to win me over."

Toby (15)

When your parents have finished dealing with their divorce, you become their number one priority. They'll try to be there to cushion the fall of any emotional spills you might have. In some cases, however, one parent can be so keen to keep you sweet that they'll do anything to make sure you turn to them first.

It's not unusual after a separation for one or both parents to feel that buying you gifts will somehow keep you happy, as well as proving how much you mean to them. It might sound cool, but ask yourself if that's really the right way for them to win your heart. What's more, there may be more to their sudden generosity than meets the eye.

Let's say your dad presents you with the latest trainers, a pair you'd be willing to sell your soul just to touch. It's a nice gesture, but what if you know it's not something your mum could ever afford to buy for you? How do you think she'll feel when you go home and show them off to her?

So if the favours and the presents start piling up, make it plain that you can't be bought. A treat's nice once in a while, but there's no need for extravagance. Let's face it, the only way your mum and dad can earn your genuine affection is through trust, respect and honesty.

After the dust has settled

"About six months after the divorce, Mum and Dad finally stopped snapping at each other. It had been a nightmare for me. I'd get back from seeing one of them only for the other to start slagging him or her off. It was as though they were still living together! I guess they both eventually realised that I was the only one getting hurt by all the abuse flying around. What makes their behaviour seem even more pointless is the fact that they quite like each other nowadays!"

Ralph (16)

Whatever the exact circumstances, your parents divorced because of differences and difficulties that couldn't be overcome. But even after the piece of paper that officially ended their marriage comes through those differences may still exist.

Many parents part company on a bad note, and their battles may continue to be conducted through you until they realise the hurt it's causing, or you speak up for yourself! On the bright side, the fact that they're not sharing the same toothbrush any more will go some way to healing old wounds. Eventually, most divorced parents will either bury the hatchet for your sake, or just agree to disagree about the things that caused them to part.

You'll know the fighting's over between your parents when you stop feeling trapped between the people you love. It will happen and the changes it brings to everyone's lives will bring on sighs of relief.

Dig out the dancing shoes, Dad

"Before Mum left, my parents rarely went out. But after the divorce, my dad surprised us all by taking up ballroom dancing! I thought he was winding me up at first, but he went to evening classes and actually became quite good at this dancing business. I'm still a bit embarrassed to admit that's what my dad does in his spare time, but I know he's happier now than ever before. Secretly, I think he fancies his dancing partner!"

Belinda (16)

No matter how badly your parents fell out throughout the divorce, there will always be a limit as to how long their conflict can last. Even if their differences remain long after the split, they each have their own lives to push on with. Fighting is no fun for anyone, and while their battles are raging it's hard for anyone to concentrate on those things in life that give them the most pleasure and help them unwind. So when the dust starts to settle both your parents will find the time to let their hair down and to concentrate on finding their feet once more.

In some cases, you may be surprised by their choice of pursuit or pastime. Often a divorce has the effect of persuading a parent to take up something that they'd never previously had the chance to do, or even thought possible while they were married! This doesn't mean that every parent goes straight from the divorce court and takes up something extreme like sky diving or bungee jumping! Just accept that whatever they choose to do it's in pursuit of happiness – something that everyone in the family deserves as a way of helping put the divorce behind them. In fact, once your mum and dad show signs of reclaiming their lives you can safely say your worries for them are over, until . . .

Who's this!

> "Mum told us about Scott on the morning before she brought him home to meet me and my sister. She told us she was very fond of him, and that she hoped things were going to work out between them. All day at school I had visions of some shadowy man with dandruff on his shoulders who wanted to take our mum from us! I was really wary about meeting him, but he wasn't at all as I had imagined. He was pretty cool, in fact, though of course we gave him a hard time to begin with. After all, isn't that how you're supposed to treat the person who might one day become your step-parent?"
>
> Harriet (15)

Often parents get divorced because one of them has formed a relationship with someone else. When this happens, not only do you find out that your mum and dad are splitting but you also have to deal with the fact that one of them loves another person! It's a double blow for you, and one that can take some getting used to. It forces you to face up to the fact that your parents are sexual beings with desires that may not have been fulfilled in marriage. Once it's all out in the open, however, at least everyone involved can set about accepting the new arrangements.

If no-one else was involved in your parents break-up, then as soon as they are separated both your mum and dad will be free to form new relationships. When it happens some time after the split you may not be as shocked. Even so, finding out that your mum and dad don't intend to remain single for the rest of their lives can still bring on mixed feelings. One part of you feels happy – even relieved – that they've found someone who makes them blush and giggle when you ask leading questions; another part of you is full doubt and concern as to whether they are doing the right thing.

It is perfectly natural to feel protective towards your parents following the break-up of their marriage. You've seen them hurt once already, so the last thing you want is to witness them make another emotional crash landing.

What time do you call this, Mum?

"The idea of my parents dating other people used to send me and my brother into fits of laughter. We used to tease them both about joining bingo clubs where all the old people hung out. I think we teased them because we didn't know how else to react."

Paddy (17)

Divorce can make you feel more protective towards your parents than ever before so when they bring home new partners it's easy to react more suspiciously than they normally do with you! In fact, just before they do the introductions they will be probably be

doing their level best to conceal their nervousness. If you've ever brought a potential boyfriend or girlfriend home to meet the parents then you'll know the score. The worries are the same, the palms clammy and the chats just as stiff and polite. This time, however, the roles have been reversed!

A replacement parent?

"When I first met Mum's new boyfriend, Stuart, I was completely struck by how similar he looked to Dad. It was only when I got to know him that I realised how different he was. He didn't have a temper for a start! It just goes to show you should never go on first impressions!" Ali (16)

When your mum or dad get involved with someone new it's almost impossible not to compare the new person to your other parent. This often stems from an anxiety about whether this person will steal your parent's affections.

Obviously, your mum and dad know better, but one way of getting over this is to find out what attracts the parent to his or her new love. If your initial impression of your parent's friend is less than flattering, then clearly you've overlooked something.

Dates don't mean marriage!

"Because Dad had walked out on Mum, I did everything in my power to make life hard for him when he first went out on a date. The first time I pretended to be sick so he had to cancel. The second and third times I just screamed at him until he called the dates off. After that I gave up, and he went out with the same woman for about a month. Then one evening he told me it was all off because she had found someone else. I couldn't help sniggering, and then both of us fell about laughing!"

Val (14)

If either of your parents embarks on a relationship try not to assume that it will automatically end up with wedding bells and a walk down the aisle. Relationships don't last forever, as your parents found out. This time around your parents may well be more cautious and just enjoy the pleasures of a romance with no strings attached.

Nobody expects you to accept your parents' new partners immediately, or to welcome them into your life with open arms right from the very first day. Instead, get to know them just as you would get to know anyone else. Try not to think of them as a replacement mum or dad. Just treat them as a close friend of one parent, who in time might grow to become a close friend of yours as well. Who knows, if things work out he or she might even become related to you by marriage!

CHAPTER EIGHT

Step-family and stuff

"When you first become a step-family it's hard not to feel a bit like a guest in someone else's house. I liked my step-mum, and my step-brother was alright too, but it took ages before I felt comfortable about stuff like stepping from the bathroom to my bedroom in just a towel!"

Nancy (14)

When you're born into a family, there's no need for you to make adjustments for everyone else. As the new arrival, others make room for you. What's more, as you have only ever known a cramped space called the womb you're unlikely to complain about being made to share a bedroom. You're even less likely to moan about the fact that everyone seems to be at your beck and call – well, for the first few years at least.

Things are a bit different if your parents split up and one of them sets up home with a new partner. This time you have to make some adjustments – you are not a new-born baby, even though at times it can seem to you like you're entering a whole new world.

But don't open your mouth and scream – you, your brothers and sisters, your parent, the new partner and his or her children are all in the same boat, so try not to rock it. Settling in takes time. You have to get to know one another, and adjust to each other's habits and lifestyles. Some things you may not be able to take for granted any more, other things will seem cooler now than they ever were before. It's all a question of learning by experience.

Where do we go from here?

"Visiting one parent on a regular basis takes planning, but there aren't any rules. One weekend I completely forgot I was due to visit my dad, and instead arranged a date with a girl. The night before, Dad phoned to check I was coming. He laughed when I told him what had happened, and said it was up to me whether or not I came to stay. He also said that if he was in my shoes, he'd go on the date! In the end, I took his advice."

Glen (15)

Even if your parents' separation was fairly straightforward, sorting out stuff like your living and visiting arrangements often involves a period of trial and error. There are many factors that go into establishing a successful new family set-up, and the situation is different for everyone.

For example, the absent parent may have moved a long way from home, and visiting them on a weekly basis may not be practical or even affordable. In other cases, it could be that the parent who has moved out needs a bit of time to settle into his or her new place before you can come round and make yourself at home.

In the beginning try out different arrangements and see which suits you all. Some you'll abandon after one go, others will seem like the most natural thing in the world. The thing is, you won't know what works until you've tried lots of options.

We'll meet again!

"Arranging to meet my mum took ages before we both fell into a routine. Either I'd be busy or she'd have something on at work. There are times when sorting a visit seems like a load of grief, and you blame your parents for forcing you into *this messy situation. Really it's just a question of making time for each other. It's worth it in the end."*

Camille (16)

There's a balance to be struck here between keeping your own life on track while adapting to any changes the separation brings. One major difference you have to accommodate is the fact that your mum or dad no longer lives under the same roof as you. Here are some questions teenagers often ask when it comes to staying in touch with the absent parent while keeping everyone in the family sweet.

When will we meet?

If the court has left it up to you and your parents to sort out visiting arrangements, then make sure you arrange a system that suits all of you. Visiting during the week, for example, may not be possible because of your school commitments or your parent's work. But if you're talking about the weekends, however, then make sure both parents understand that it's a precious time for all of you, and that the arrangement needs to be flexible. If there's a major party planned for the Saturday night, for instance, and missing out is going to make you miserable, then find out if you could postpone the visit.

It's also worth remembering that although your mum or dad will always want to see you, sometimes things may crop up in their diaries that will mean rearranging your stay.

Visiting an absent parent is all about wanting to see each other and enjoying your time together. Sometimes you may wish to increase your number of visits; other times you might both want a break! Compromise, and keep a supple system to which all of you can adapt in accommodating the giddy social whirl that surrounds your life!

Where shall we meet?

Arranging a time is one thing, sorting out a place is another! Often this is a question that arises just after your parents have separated. Again, there are many factors to watch out for. If your mum or your dad has left home before making any permanent plans about where he or she is going to live, then for a while you may have to meet in public places like the park, the library or town centre. If your parents no longer get on then the absent parent may not be able to come and pick you up, in which case there are travel arrangements to be made.

In other situations, the absent parent may live so far away that it's only practical to meet half-way. Sometimes, when the absent parent doesn't have a suitable place for you to meet up, there are centres you can visit where you can relax and spend time together. (For more details, see Chapter Ten.)

What will we do together?

If you don't see the absent parent very often, it's easy

to think that you have to catch up on lost time by squeezing in as many non-stop activities as possible. But enjoying your time together doesn't depend upon how many movies you can squeeze into your stay!

Doing stuff you don't usually do together can eventually seem a bit false. It really doesn't take a special event to make your visit special too.

Sure, it's good to plan something in advance once in a while, but just spending time under the same roof with each other can make a visit worthwhile. Find out what you'd each like to do in advance of your stay, and if you want to lounge in front of the TV while your mum or dad mows the lawn, then do it!

What about Christmas and birthdays?

There are times in the calendar when families traditionally get together. If your parents live in two different homes, however, it can make things difficult. Trying to please both sides over stuff like Easter, Christmas and birthdays may be impossible, especially if your parents live miles apart. Basically, the trick is to plan ahead. Divide your time fairly and try to arrange things so that you and your parents are happy. But it is almost impossible to please everyone all the time, and trying to do so will only leave you miserable.

Switching sides?

"Things didn't work out as planned when I went to live with Dad. Because he was constantly away at work I had no-one to talk to. Eventually he realised I was unhappy, and said it was okay for me to move back with Mum. He was great about it, but I had no idea he'd be so understanding. I suppose I only had to ask."

Charles (14)

Even if your mum and dad were certain that divorce was the best way forwards, the way it affects your life may not always feel right for you. Choosing which parent you should live with is a hard decision to make, and often there is no absolutely right choice as you're bound to feel bad for the parent you've opted not to live with. Also, once the choice has been made there will be moments when you think things would be better if you were living on the other side of the fence.

When a parent is absent you may not get to see his or her grumpy side. Therefore it's easy to imagine that living with that parent would be fantastic. If you've had a row with the parent you live with, for instance, try not to fall for the fantasy that the other parent would be more understanding or more forgiving. This is just wishful thinking, and really things would be just the same no matter which one you lived with. You might think the grass is greener at the other home, but in reality there are bound to be few a weeds in both gardens!

We all make mistakes and some people do come to realise that they'd be genuinely happier living with their other parent. If this happens, and you really believe it would be better switching sides, then talk to your mum or dad about the situation. You may feel awkward or ashamed to admit you're unhappy living with him or her, but being honest is the only way this problem is going to be solved.

Besides, it's not as if you're saying you love one parent more than the other. It just comes down to a question of which living arrangement makes your life easier to lead.

Don't set your heart on making the change because it may not be practical for your mum or dad to take you on at their place.

What's more, you might find that a chat with the parent you live with actually clears up the problems that made you first think about switching over!

Single parents, fantasy fathers and wicked stepmothers

"I wanted Dad to be happy, but part of me didn't want him to find someone new."

Siri (16)

Not everyone whose parents have separated finds themselves living in a stepfamily situation straight away. If no-one else played a part in the break-up of your mum and dad's marriage then, in all likelihood, you'll be living with just one parent for a while. Even though nobody new has come into your family, life with a single mum or dad can still bring many changes to the household. The parent you remain with will probably find adjusting to the new situation as hard as you, and for that parent, post-divorce life means that for much of the time he or she has to take on the role of both parents. He or she is now faced with all the responsibilities and chores that were once shared.

Often this means that you'll have to help out a bit. Perhaps you'll have to begin washing your own clothes or picking up a younger sibling from school. It might seem like a drag, but your mum or dad will be less stressed therefore making your life easier.

In time, you'll get used to this new family role. However, you should be aware that it's a role that changes if your one-parent family is ever transformed into a step-family.

One parent, two roles

"My dad sometimes comes back from work, changes out of his suit and gets straight into doing the dusting. He says it's a way of winding down!"

Joyce, (15)

Living with just your mum or dad means that problems can't be solved by simply turning to the other parent. You can always cry down the telephone or send a letter to the absent parent listing all your grievances,

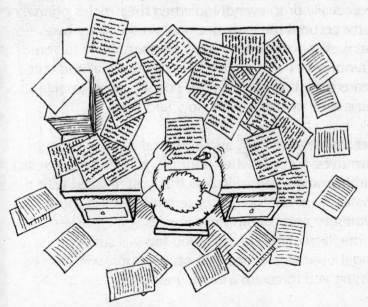

but you should also be aware of the pressures facing the parent you're living with. He or she will be doing their utmost to make everyone happy, so try not fly off the handle the moment things don't go your way.

If something doesn't seem right or fair to you, then

talk the problem through. Don't automatically assume that if the absent parent was around, he or she would automatically come down on your side.

Once your parents have parted company their social life may also change – often beyond recognition! Whereas before they may not have had many interests outside their marriage, your mum and dad are now free agents once again. Just like you, they are entitled to meet new people, go out on dates and even fall head over heels in love again! Unlike you, however, they can't really drop everything when their mates phone, or party on until the early hours when the fancy takes them. As a parent, they have a responsibility to you, your brothers and sisters. So in return for all the time and energy they give over to you, it's good to give them a bit of space every now and then.

Get the balance right and everyone can get on with their lives. It's only when your mum or dad comes back with someone special in tow that you're faced with the possibility of another family rethink. Just like those who witnessed one parent move in with someone else immediately after the split, you too will suddenly have to get used to the idea that other people will soon be joining you to create a whole new nest!

You're not my real parent!

"I found it really difficult when Mark moved in after the divorce. I felt like he'd stepped into Dad's shoes, even though I knew he was really a nice guy."

Imogen (16)

When someone new comes into your mum or dad's life, don't make the mistake of assuming that he or she is trying to take the place of the absent parent. Get to know him or her on the basis that this person is the one who can give your mum or dad companionship, comfort and security. Yes, they will be in the same bed, and often this is an uncomfortable reality to accept, but if being together in this way makes your parent happy then it can only mean a happier house all round. In time, they may get married, but it's not compulsory for them to do so. The relationship may end long before talk of wedding bells begins. Sometimes, when it's evident how strongly one parent feels for their new partner, it's easy to feel under some kind of pressure yourself to accept him or her into your life. The thing is that the parent concerned won't be expecting you to get on like a house on fire from day one.

If the new partner was involved in the break-up of your parents' marriage it can be really very hard indeed for you to instantly welcome them into the family. Whatever your situation, it's important to remember that however deeply your parent falls in love, your mum or dad's feelings for you won't change one tiny bit.

It's not uncommon to start off feeling slightly resentful of any new partner. Some become jealous, or even feel rejected by their parent, simply because that parent is spending lots of time with his or her new love. When it comes to dealing with these emotions try to accept that the existence of your parent's new partner basically signals the end of any secret dream, hope or fantasy you might have had of your mum and dad getting back together. Once you've come to terms with the reality of the situation you can set about appreciating that the new partner is someone who makes your mum or dad smile!

EVERYTHING'S FINE! ALRIGHT! NOW BOG OFF!

If you end up sharing the same house, however, this new person may have standards and rules that you've never come across or that seem unfair to you. Whatever your differences, and these will arise until you know each other better, it's important to get them out in the open. If you feel awkward raising personal matters like this with your mum or dad's partner, then talk to your parent alone. Sometimes it actually helps to look at the situation from the new person's point of view. He or she, of course, wants the relationship to work, and will be very sensitive to the fact that the absent parent may have done things differently. But it's up to you to be aware that this doesn't necessarily mean that there's a right or a wrong way; often it's just a question of finding the middle ground.

The worst thing you can do is to keep quiet and brood over any problems that arise between you and your parent's new partner. While their relationship develops, don't spend your time building up a negative picture. At the same time, if you're missing the absent parent it's easy to think of him or her as perfect. And then, in your mind, you have transformed a perfectly nice person into a clichéd wicked step-parent!

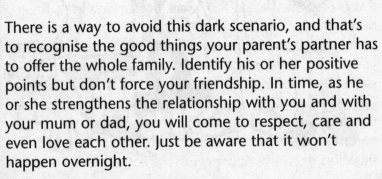

There is a way to avoid this dark scenario, and that's to recognise the good things your parent's partner has to offer the whole family. Identify his or her positive points but don't force your friendship. In time, as he or she strengthens the relationship with you and with your mum or dad, you will come to respect, care and even love each other. Just be aware that it won't happen overnight.

One family?

"Sarah wasn't my idea of the perfect wife for my dad as she was much younger than my mum. But the day before Dad and Sarah married, Dad sat down with me and spelled out why she made him happy, and that was good enough for me."

Elizabeth (15)

Just because your parents have divorced it doesn't mean their belief in the idea of marriage has hit the rocks too. In Britain, around half of all people who divorce remarry within five years. For some it comes as a surprise to hear that their mum or dad are planning to get hitched again. After all the strife the last marriage caused, many find it hard to understand why their parents would want to risk it again. The thing is, people enter into a marriage with the best intentions in the world. They believe it will strengthen their relationship and provide a solid foundation on which a family can grow and spread its wings.

If a remarriage is on the cards, it's likely that your mum or dad will talk to you before broadcasting the news from the rooftops. Your parent will want to be sure you understand that no ring on any finger or change in surname will alter the relationship with you, or his or her love for you. Whatever feelings you have towards the prospective step-parent, always be aware that he or she won't ever replace the real parent. You don't necessarily have to call them 'Mum' or 'Dad' and nothing will change how often you get to see the real thing! One change any remarriage will make to your life however, is that your mum or dad are creating a whole new living arrangement!

Step forward the step-family!

"At Dad's wedding I was introduced to lots of people – they all turned out to be my new relations by marriage. There were step-aunts and step-uncles, and my new

step-mum's cousin also managed to work out our connection!
By the end of the day I thought my head was going to spin off!
It's nice having such a big step-family, but you never forget
how much your real family means to you."

Bryn (15)

A step-family is created when one of your parents
remarries. As well as the lucky person becoming your
step-parent, any children he or she has will then
become your step-brothers or step-sisters. It sounds
fairly simple until you start to think of all the different
relationship combinations that can be formed when
two family trees are joined!

No two step-family arrangements are ever the same;
like diamonds they are totally unique. Some aspects
of this new life you'll love, though there will always be
flaws. If there are lots of children involved, for
example, then you might find yourself becoming a
master in the art of making the most of a shared
living space. Alternatively, it could be that you
discover a soul-mate in your step-brother or -sister.
What is common to all new step-families, however, is
the fact that everyone will need time to adapt and
settle. With understanding and respect for everyone
concerned, a step-family can work as one.

A step in the right direction

"My mum and my step-mum have become good
friends over the years. I guess this is because they
have so much in common! The main link of course is

Dad, and often they joke about his annoying habits like leaving toe-nail clippings in the bath. Sometimes they disagree about what's best for me, but whatever their decision I know both of them have my interests at heart."

Heidi (15)

You may already have a strong relationship with your new step-mum or step-dad. Perhaps she or he has been living with you and your parent for some time, in which case the step-parent may already seem like one of the family long before the wedding takes place. In other instances it may take some time for you to appreciate the family role this new person will play.

It may help you get used to the idea of having a step-parent by thinking about the differences he or she will make to your family situation. Okay, so once your parent and his or her partner are married, you might have less time with your mum or dad, but that also means less time nagging you! Your household chores may be reduced now that there's an extra pair of hands about the house, and you may feel more secure having two adults under the same roof.

Even though the new set-up may mean some sacrifices, a step-parent can bring many good things to your family; he or she might come with children. Whether this is an advantage or not, only time will tell!

Step-brothers, step-sisters and new sprogs!

"The great thing about my step-sister is the fact that she's got loads of really good-looking mates who are always calling round at our house!"

Brooke (17)

If you have any brothers or sisters, then you'll know that sometimes you get on brilliantly and at other times you're the worst of enemies. Well, things are exactly the same when it comes to step-brothers or step-sisters, so don't judge them on your first impressions.

Many people have high expectations when they first meet their step-siblings. They hope to become instant friends, united by the common link that their parents have formed a relationship. In reality, when you find yourself thrown into the step-family melting pot things often don't work out as hoped. Living in the same house together can mean that people annoy each other and tempers are brought to the boil.

Getting along together

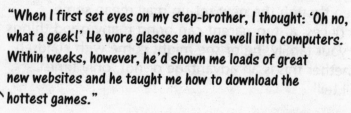

"When I first set eyes on my step-brother, I thought: 'Oh no, what a geek!' He wore glasses and was well into computers. Within weeks, however, he'd shown me loads of great new websites and he taught me how to download the hottest games."

Chester (16)

To get off on the right foot with any new step-brothers or step-sisters, don't make any assumptions about what they might be like. Instead, spend a bit of time getting to know them. Even though age differences will play a part in how much you hang around together, be tolerant over differences in attitudes, opinions, likes and dislikes. After all, you've grown up in different homes so it would be a miracle if you had identical tastes in everything. Providing you respect each other as individuals and make some space for one another when it's needed, then you'll get on fine.

One thing to watch out for: don't be anything more than just friends with your step-sibling. If you're of similar age then strong sexual feelings can develop, especially as you're forced into a degree of intimacy by living under the same roof. No matter how attracted you are to each other, forming any sexual relationship really isn't a great idea because of the problems it can cause in the future. Apart from the grief getting together would cause your parents, imagine how difficult life would be if you split up but still had to live together! Be sensible about this issue and don't be tempted into something you are likely to regret!

And baby makes . . .?

"I was worried when Dad and my step-mum announced they were having a baby. It wasn't the idea of my dad being a father to someone else, I was more concerned about whether I'd have to chip in and do stuff like changing nappies!"

Ewan (14)

If there's one thing that can unite a step-family, it's a new baby. It may not seem this way when the new arrival first hits your home and everyone has to squeeze up to make room. Then there's the screaming sessions to consider, and the fact that your parent and step-parent have turned into gibbering zombies in their dedication to the ever-changing nappy routine. Yet like everything that follows a divorce, you will need a period to adjust to the changes and settle down. Having a new baby around is a bit like getting used to using an extension on your house. In the beginning you feel a bit weird about something that hasn't always been there, but over time you'll wonder how you ever got on without it.

If you feel jealous of all the attention your new half-brother or half-sister is receiving, consider the fact that all babies take up lots of parental time and energy. If your parent and step-parent are spending less time with you it doesn't mean they love you any less, it's just that unlike the new sprog you're potty trained!

CHAPTER NINE

My parents are divorced, so what!

"Ten years ago my world fell to pieces when my mum and dad split up. At the time I thought things would never be the same again. Looking back I'd say they actually got better! Before, during and after the divorce I talked to my parents more openly than ever before, and learned a thing or two about how relationships work. I became more responsible and took greater control over my life. In turn, both my parents learned to trust me, which meant I could do things without them worrying needlessly or fussing over me. I was fifteen at the time, but from the moment they split up both of them stopped treating me like a little kid and instead talked to me as a young adult."

Simon (25)

Family break-up is all about change. Nobody wants it to happen to their parents, but when they make the decision to split you have to adapt and move on with them. It's never an easy transition.

Divorce doesn't always solve your parents' problems and some teenagers find the emotional impact has a negative affect on other areas of their lives. Yet as so many young people have testified in this book, with help and understanding there are valuable lessons to be learned from the experience.

Above all, divorce teaches us about love in all its different guises. You see the downside when your mum and dad separate, which is an important lesson in itself, but you also come to recognise how strong and enduring love can be between parents and their children. In fact, when parents make the break from each other, the bonds with their children often grow much stronger. Your communication with them can improve, and with this comes honesty and trust – all in the name of love.

Then there's the kind of love that grows from scratch within a step-family, and let's not forget the love that grows between friends. Now you may not love your best mate in the romantic sense, but when parents split, a friend can provide the comfort, support and distraction you need. Like it or not, that's love! Learn to recognise its value, fragility and strengths, and it can only help when you come to form future relationships.

Of course, there are emotional knocks to take when your parents split up, but if you deal with them properly and positively you'll come through the experience with wisdom on your side, ready to take on the world. After all, you still have your own life to lead. What's more it won't be long before you get the chance to spread your wings and fly from the family nest – whatever state it's in! Who knows, one day you may find yourself giving out advice to teenagers caught in the middle of their parents' divorce. So good luck, don't paint your room black and stay smiling!

Resources

Through every stage of your parents' separation and divorce it's absolutely vital that you find someone you trust to talk to. Without being able to voice your feelings and fears it's easy to end up anxious and confused about your past, present and future.

Ideally, your parents should be the first port of call

when the problems pile up. However at a time when both of them are trying to deal with their own feelings about the divorce, they may not be sympathetic listeners or able to give you sound, balanced advice. Alternatively you might simply feel too awkward about discussing your feelings with them. In this case, you may find it easier to open your heart to an outsider – someone who isn't emotionally involved – like a teacher, a good mate, a family friend or a trained, professional counsellor.

Whatever your worries, help is always at hand for you, your brothers and sisters, and also for your mum and dad.

Helplines

Careline
Tel: 0181 514 1177
For anyone who wants
to talk through their
worries, problems and fears with a trained counsellor.

ChildLine
Freephone: 0800 1111
Trained counsellors provide advice for children on any issue that troubles them. Calls are free and won't appear on the phone bill. You can also write to ChildLine: Freepost 1111, London N1 0BR (no stamp needed).

Samaritans
Tel: 0345 909090
A 24-hour confidential telephone service for anyone in despair.

Parentline Plus
Tel: 0808 800 2222
A UK registered charity offering support to anyone
parenting a child, including step-parents and foster
parents. (Good for adults in need of help too!)

Organisations

These organisations can be contacted by letter or by
phone. Some offer their help and advice just to
children or their parents, others deal with the whole
family on special issues.

Child Poverty Action Group
4th Floor, 1-5 Bath Street,
London EC1V 9PY
Tel: 0207 253 3406
www.cpag.org.uk
Offers publications on benefits available for low-
income families.

Children's Legal Centre
University of Essex,
Wivenhoe Park,
Colchester, Essex CO4 3SQ
Tel: 01206 873820
www.childrenlegalcentre.com
The centre offers a telephone advice service between
10.00am and 12.00pm, and between 2.00pm and
5.00pm, Monday to Friday.

The Children's Society
Edward Rudolf House,
69-85 Margery Street, London WC1X OJL
Tel: 0207 837 4299
www.the-childrens-society.org.uk
Offers support to children and families under pressure.

Gingerbread
16-17 Clerkenwell Close
London EC1R 0AA
Tel: 0800 018 4318
A national self-help
association for
one-parent families,
offering a network
of local groups and
a range of advice
leaflets.

National Council for One Parent Families
255 Kentish Town Road,
London NW5 2LX
Tel: 0800 018 5026
www.oneparentfamilies.org.uk
Free information service providing help for all one-parent families.

Network of Access and Child Contact Centres
St Andrew's with Castlegate URC,
Goldsmith Street,
Nottingham NG1 5JT
Tel: 0115 948 4557
Email: contact@naccc.org.uk
Provides details of a network of centres offering a neutral, comfortable and safe environment where children can meet with an absent parent.

One Parent Family (Scotland)
13 Gayfield Square,
Edinburgh, Scotland EH1 3NX
Tel: 0131 556 3899
www.opfs.org.uk
Offers advice, information and a counselling service for lone parents.

Scottish Child Law Centre
23 Buccleuch Place
Edinburgh
Scotland
Tel: 0131 667 6333

Relate National Marriage Guidance
Herbert Gray College,
Little Church Street,
Rugby, Warwickshire CV21 3AP
Tel: 01788 573241
An organisation that helps adults overcome marital problems. Relate also offers advice to couples whose relationship cannot be saved. The national headquarters in Rugby will provide details of your nearest Relate centre.

Index

Wise Guides:
helping you deal with whatever life throws at you

Bullying
Michele Elliott

Drugs
Anita Naik

Eating
Anita Naik

Exam Skills
Kate Brookes

Family Break-up
Matt Whyman

Periods
Charlotte Owen

Personal Safety
Anita Naik

Self-Esteem
Anita Naik

Sex
Anita Naik

Wise Guide

SELF ESTEEM

Anita Naik

What are you?
Positive bod or negative nerd?
Do you find it hard to take compliments?
Do you never take risks in case you make
a fool of yourself?
Then you need to respect yourself!

Anita Naik gives loads of helpful tips on
how to feel better about yourself and
build your self-esteem. Get in touch with
that positive bod that's just waiting to be
let loose on the world!

Wise Guide

DRUGS

Anita Naik

What are drugs?
What do they do to your mind –
and your body?
Are you under pressure to take drugs?
Do you have friends who already do?
What are the risks – and how should
you deal with them?

Alcohol and amphetamines, tobacco and
cannabis, solvents and steroids – know
the realities and explode the myths with
this essential wise guide.

BULLYING

Michele Elliott

Nearly everyone is bullied at some point in their life. But what exactly does bullying mean? Are there practical things you can do to stop it? How do you deal with your anger and frustration? How can you learn to make friends and respect yourself? If you're a bully, can you ever change your behaviour?

Don't suffer in silence. Learn how to beat the bullies and restore your self-esteem with this essential wise guide.

Wise Guide

PERSONAL SAFETY

Anita Naik

Are you street smart? Do you step outside feeling confident and secure?

Whatever your outlook one thing is for certain, personal safety is something you can't ignore.

This essential wise guide shows you how to look after yourself when you are out on the street or on the net. Learn how to be more aware of what's going on around you and how to react if you find yourself in a risky situation.